50 Island Dessert Recipes for Home

By: Kelly Johnson

Table of Contents

- Pina Colada Cake
- Mango Sticky Rice
- Coconut Macaroons
- Rum Raisin Ice Cream
- Passion Fruit Sorbet
- Tropical Fruit Tart
- Hummingbird Cake
- Key Lime Pie
- Banana Foster
- Pineapple Upside-Down Cake
- Coconut Panna Cotta
- Mango Coconut Rice Pudding
- Island Coconut Cream Pie
- Jamaican Jerk Brownies
- Guava Cheesecake
- Papaya Lime Parfait
- Taro Root Cake
- Sweet Plantain Fritters
- Caribbean Pineapple Flan
- Rum-Soaked Banana Bread
- Passion Fruit Pavlova
- Mango Chia Seed Pudding
- Coconut Pineapple Muffins
- Tropical Trifle
- Caramelized Banana Tarte Tatin
- Pineapple and Coconut Smoothie Bowl
- Island Spice Cupcakes
- Tropical Fruit Salad with Lime Mint Dressing
- Coconut Rice Krispies Treats
- Mango and Sticky Rice Spring Rolls
- Rum Punch Gelato
- Papaya Coconut Cheesecake Bars

- Pineapple Gingerbread Cookies
- Caribbean Chocolate Cake
- Mango Lime Bars
- Coconut Lime Cheesecake
- Tropical Sorbet Sundaes
- Spiced Plantain Muffins
- Rum and Raisin Bread Pudding
- Pineapple Coconut Bars
- Mango Sorbet Float
- Coconut Almond Energy Balls
- Passion Fruit Meringue Pie
- Tropical Fruit Crumble
- Pina Colada Cupcakes
- Papaya Sorbet
- Tropical Coconut Flan
- Mango and Coconut Panna Cotta
- Caribbean Sweet Potato Pie
- Pineapple Coconut Ice Cream Sandwiches

Pina Colada Cake

Ingredients:

For the Cake:

- 1 1/2 cups all-purpose flour
- 1 1/2 teaspoons baking powder
- 1/2 teaspoon baking soda
- 1/4 teaspoon salt
- 1/2 cup unsalted butter, at room temperature
- 1 cup granulated sugar
- 2 large eggs
- 1/2 cup crushed pineapple, drained
- 1/2 cup shredded coconut (sweetened or unsweetened)
- 1/2 cup coconut milk
- 1/4 cup rum (or use additional coconut milk for a non-alcoholic version)
- 1 teaspoon vanilla extract

For the Coconut Frosting:

- 1/2 cup unsalted butter, at room temperature
- 2 cups powdered sugar
- 1/4 cup coconut milk
- 1 teaspoon vanilla extract
- 1/2 cup shredded coconut, toasted (for garnish)

For the Pineapple Filling (optional):

- 1 cup crushed pineapple, drained
- 1/4 cup granulated sugar
- 1 tablespoon cornstarch

Instructions:

1. **Prepare the Cake:**
   - Preheat your oven to 350°F (175°C). Grease and flour an 8-inch round cake pan or two 8-inch round cake pans.
   - In a medium bowl, whisk together flour, baking powder, baking soda, and salt.
   - In a large bowl, cream the butter and granulated sugar together until light and fluffy.
   - Beat in the eggs, one at a time, until fully incorporated.
   - Mix in the crushed pineapple, shredded coconut, coconut milk, rum (if using), and vanilla extract.

- Gradually add the dry ingredients to the wet ingredients, mixing just until combined.
- Pour the batter into the prepared cake pan(s) and smooth the top.
- Bake for 25-30 minutes, or until a toothpick inserted into the center comes out clean.
- Allow the cake to cool in the pan for 10 minutes, then transfer to a wire rack to cool completely.

2. **Prepare the Pineapple Filling (optional):**
   - In a small saucepan, combine crushed pineapple, granulated sugar, and cornstarch.
   - Cook over medium heat, stirring constantly, until the mixture thickens (about 5-7 minutes).
   - Remove from heat and let cool.

3. **Prepare the Coconut Frosting:**
   - In a large bowl, beat the butter until creamy.
   - Gradually add the powdered sugar, coconut milk, and vanilla extract, beating until smooth and fluffy.
   - If the frosting is too thick, add a little more coconut milk; if too thin, add more powdered sugar.

4. **Assemble the Cake:**
   - If using two cake layers, place one layer on a serving plate and spread the pineapple filling (if using) evenly over it.
   - Place the second layer on top.
   - Frost the top and sides of the cake with the coconut frosting.
   - Garnish with toasted shredded coconut.

5. **Serve:**
   - Slice and serve the cake. Enjoy the tropical flavors of this Pina Colada Cake with family and friends!

This Pina Colada Cake is a fun and delicious way to enjoy the flavors of a classic tropical cocktail in dessert form.

Mango Sticky Rice

Ingredients:

For the Sticky Rice:

- 1 cup glutinous (sticky) rice
- 1 1/4 cups coconut milk
- 1/2 cup granulated sugar
- 1/4 teaspoon salt

For the Mango:

- 2 ripe mangoes, peeled and sliced

For the Topping (optional):

- 2 tablespoons toasted sesame seeds or shredded coconut
- Fresh mint leaves for garnish (optional)

Instructions:

1. **Prepare the Sticky Rice:**
   - Rinse the sticky rice under cold water until the water runs clear. This helps remove excess starch.
   - Soak the rice in cold water for at least 30 minutes, or up to 2 hours.
   - Drain the rice and place it in a steamer basket lined with cheesecloth or parchment paper.
   - Steam the rice over simmering water for about 20-25 minutes, or until the rice is tender and translucent.
2. **Prepare the Coconut Sauce:**
   - In a medium saucepan, combine coconut milk, sugar, and salt.
   - Heat over medium heat, stirring constantly, until the sugar is dissolved and the mixture is heated through. Do not let it boil.
   - Reserve about 1/4 cup of the coconut sauce for drizzling over the finished dish.
3. **Combine Rice and Coconut Sauce:**
   - Once the sticky rice is cooked, transfer it to a large bowl.
   - Stir in the majority of the coconut sauce (leaving the reserved 1/4 cup for later use) until the rice is evenly coated and the mixture is well combined.
   - Allow the rice to sit for about 10 minutes to absorb the flavors.
4. **Prepare the Mango:**
   - Peel and slice the mangoes into thin strips or bite-sized pieces.
5. **Assemble the Dessert:**
   - Spoon a portion of the sticky rice onto serving plates.

- Arrange the mango slices on the side of the sticky rice.
- Drizzle the reserved coconut sauce over the rice and mango.

6. **Garnish and Serve:**
    - Sprinkle with toasted sesame seeds or shredded coconut, if desired.
    - Garnish with fresh mint leaves if you like.
    - Serve warm or at room temperature.

Enjoy your Mango Sticky Rice, a beautifully balanced dessert that pairs the richness of coconut milk with the sweet, juicy freshness of ripe mangoes.

Coconut Macaroons

Ingredients:

- 4 cups sweetened shredded coconut
- 1 can (14 oz) sweetened condensed milk
- 1 teaspoon vanilla extract
- 2 large egg whites
- 1/4 teaspoon salt
- 1/2 cup semi-sweet chocolate chips (optional, for dipping)

Instructions:

1. **Preheat Oven:**
    - Preheat your oven to 325°F (165°C). Line a baking sheet with parchment paper or a silicone baking mat.
2. **Prepare the Coconut Mixture:**
    - In a large bowl, combine the shredded coconut, sweetened condensed milk, and vanilla extract. Stir until well mixed.
3. **Whip the Egg Whites:**
    - In a separate bowl, using an electric mixer, beat the egg whites with the salt until stiff peaks form (about 2-3 minutes).
4. **Fold in the Egg Whites:**
    - Gently fold the whipped egg whites into the coconut mixture until just combined. Be careful not to overmix; you want to maintain the fluffiness of the egg whites.
5. **Form the Macaroons:**
    - Use a spoon or a small cookie scoop to drop heaping tablespoons of the mixture onto the prepared baking sheet, spacing them about 1 inch apart. You can also shape them into small mounds if desired.
6. **Bake:**
    - Bake in the preheated oven for 15-20 minutes, or until the macaroons are golden brown on the edges and set in the center.
7. **Cool:**
    - Allow the macaroons to cool on the baking sheet for about 5 minutes before transferring them to a wire rack to cool completely.
8. **Optional Chocolate Dip:**
    - If you'd like to add a chocolate coating, melt the chocolate chips in a microwave-safe bowl in 30-second intervals, stirring between each interval, until smooth.
    - Dip the bottoms of the cooled macaroons into the melted chocolate and place them back on the parchment paper to let the chocolate set.

Enjoy your Coconut Macaroons as a sweet treat for any occasion! They're perfect with a cup of tea or coffee and make a great addition to any dessert table.

Rum Raisin Ice Cream

Ingredients:

For the Raisins:

- 1/2 cup raisins
- 1/4 cup dark rum

For the Ice Cream Base:

- 1 cup whole milk
- 2 cups heavy cream
- 3/4 cup granulated sugar
- 1/2 cup packed brown sugar
- 5 large egg yolks
- 1 teaspoon vanilla extract
- 1/4 teaspoon salt

Instructions:

1. **Soak the Raisins:**
    - In a small bowl, combine the raisins and dark rum. Let them soak for at least 1 hour, or overnight if possible, so that the raisins absorb the rum and plump up.
2. **Prepare the Ice Cream Base:**
    - In a medium saucepan, heat the milk and heavy cream over medium heat until it just begins to simmer. Do not let it boil.
    - In a separate bowl, whisk together the granulated sugar, brown sugar, and egg yolks until pale and slightly thickened.
    - Slowly pour about 1 cup of the hot milk mixture into the egg yolk mixture, whisking constantly to temper the eggs.
    - Return the egg mixture to the saucepan with the remaining milk mixture. Cook over medium heat, stirring constantly with a wooden spoon or heatproof spatula, until the mixture thickens enough to coat the back of the spoon. This should take about 5-7 minutes. Do not let it boil.
3. **Strain and Chill:**
    - Remove the saucepan from the heat and stir in the vanilla extract and salt.
    - Strain the mixture through a fine-mesh sieve into a clean bowl to remove any cooked egg bits.
    - Let the mixture cool to room temperature, then cover and refrigerate for at least 4 hours, or overnight, until thoroughly chilled.
4. **Churn the Ice Cream:**
    - Pour the chilled ice cream base into an ice cream maker and churn according to the manufacturer's instructions.

    - In the last few minutes of churning, add the soaked raisins along with any remaining rum.
5. **Freeze:**
    - Transfer the churned ice cream to a lidded container and freeze for at least 2 hours to firm up before serving.
6. **Serve:**
    - Scoop the Rum Raisin Ice Cream into bowls or cones and enjoy!

This homemade Rum Raisin Ice Cream is rich, creamy, and full of flavor, with the rum-soaked raisins adding a delightful burst of sweetness and spice.

Passion Fruit Sorbet

Ingredients:

- 1 cup passion fruit juice (about 6-8 fresh passion fruits or store-bought juice)
- 1 cup granulated sugar
- 1 cup water
- 1 tablespoon lemon juice (optional, for added tartness)
- 1/4 teaspoon salt

Instructions:

1. **Prepare the Simple Syrup:**
   - In a medium saucepan, combine the sugar and water.
   - Heat over medium heat, stirring constantly, until the sugar is fully dissolved. This will create a simple syrup.
   - Remove from heat and let the syrup cool to room temperature.
2. **Combine Ingredients:**
   - In a large bowl, mix the cooled simple syrup with the passion fruit juice.
   - If using, stir in the lemon juice and salt. The lemon juice adds a bit more tartness, which enhances the flavor of the sorbet.
3. **Chill the Mixture:**
   - Cover the mixture and refrigerate for at least 2 hours, or until thoroughly chilled. Chilling the mixture helps it freeze more evenly.
4. **Churn the Sorbet:**
   - Pour the chilled mixture into an ice cream maker and churn according to the manufacturer's instructions. This usually takes about 20-30 minutes, or until the sorbet has a soft-serve consistency.
5. **Freeze:**
   - Transfer the churned sorbet to a lidded container and freeze for at least 2 hours to firm up before serving.
6. **Serve:**
   - Scoop the Passion Fruit Sorbet into bowls or glasses and enjoy!

Tips:

- **Fresh Passion Fruit:** If using fresh passion fruits, cut them in half and scoop out the pulp. Strain the pulp through a fine-mesh sieve to extract the juice, pressing with the back of a spoon to get as much juice as possible. You should get about 1 cup of juice from 6-8 passion fruits.
- **No Ice Cream Maker?** If you don't have an ice cream maker, pour the mixture into a shallow dish and freeze. Every 30 minutes, stir the mixture with a fork to break up ice crystals until the sorbet is fully frozen and fluffy.

Enjoy this Passion Fruit Sorbet as a refreshing and exotic treat that's sure to delight your taste buds!

Tropical Fruit Tart

Ingredients:

For the Tart Crust:

- 1 1/2 cups all-purpose flour
- 1/2 cup granulated sugar
- 1/4 teaspoon salt
- 1/2 cup cold unsalted butter, cubed
- 1 large egg yolk
- 2 tablespoons ice water (more if needed)

For the Pastry Cream:

- 1 cup whole milk
- 1/2 cup granulated sugar
- 3 large egg yolks
- 2 tablespoons cornstarch
- 2 tablespoons unsalted butter
- 1 teaspoon vanilla extract

For the Topping:

- 1 cup fresh mango, peeled and diced
- 1 cup fresh pineapple, peeled and diced
- 1 cup fresh kiwi, peeled and sliced
- 1/2 cup passion fruit pulp or other tropical fruit (optional)
- 1/4 cup apricot jam (for glaze, optional)

Instructions:

1. **Prepare the Tart Crust:**
   - In a medium bowl, whisk together flour, sugar, and salt.
   - Cut in the cold butter using a pastry cutter or your fingers until the mixture resembles coarse crumbs.
   - Mix in the egg yolk and add ice water, 1 tablespoon at a time, until the dough just comes together.
   - Form the dough into a disk, wrap in plastic wrap, and refrigerate for at least 30 minutes.
2. **Preheat Oven and Prepare Tart Pan:**
   - Preheat your oven to 375°F (190°C).
   - On a lightly floured surface, roll out the dough to fit a 9-inch tart pan. Press the dough into the pan and trim any excess.

- Prick the bottom of the crust with a fork to prevent bubbling.
3. **Blind Bake the Crust:**
   - Line the crust with parchment paper and fill with pie weights or dried beans.
   - Bake for 15 minutes, then remove the weights and parchment paper.
   - Bake for an additional 5-7 minutes, or until the crust is golden brown. Let cool completely.
4. **Prepare the Pastry Cream:**
   - In a medium saucepan, heat the milk until it just begins to simmer.
   - In a bowl, whisk together sugar, egg yolks, and cornstarch until smooth.
   - Slowly pour the hot milk into the egg mixture, whisking constantly.
   - Return the mixture to the saucepan and cook over medium heat, whisking constantly, until it thickens and begins to bubble.
   - Remove from heat and stir in butter and vanilla extract. Let cool to room temperature, then chill in the refrigerator.
5. **Assemble the Tart:**
   - Spread the chilled pastry cream evenly over the cooled tart crust.
   - Arrange the diced mango, pineapple, kiwi, and passion fruit pulp (if using) on top of the pastry cream in a decorative pattern.
6. **Glaze (Optional):**
   - If using, heat the apricot jam in a small saucepan until melted and smooth.
   - Brush the apricot glaze over the fruit to give it a shiny finish.
7. **Serve:**
   - Refrigerate the tart until ready to serve.
   - Slice and enjoy the vibrant flavors of the tropical fruit tart!

This Tropical Fruit Tart is a refreshing and visually stunning dessert that's perfect for any occasion. The combination of a buttery crust, creamy filling, and fresh fruit is sure to be a hit!

Hummingbird Cake

Ingredients:

For the Cake:

- 1 1/2 cups granulated sugar
- 1/2 cup packed brown sugar
- 3 cups all-purpose flour
- 1 teaspoon baking powder
- 1/2 teaspoon baking soda
- 1/2 teaspoon salt
- 1 teaspoon ground cinnamon
- 1/2 teaspoon ground nutmeg
- 1/2 teaspoon ground allspice
- 1/2 cup vegetable oil
- 3 large eggs
- 1 teaspoon vanilla extract
- 1 cup mashed ripe bananas (about 2 medium bananas)
- 1 cup crushed pineapple, drained
- 1/2 cup chopped pecans
- 1/2 cup shredded coconut (optional)

For the Cream Cheese Frosting:

- 8 oz cream cheese, softened
- 1/2 cup unsalted butter, softened
- 4 cups powdered sugar
- 1 teaspoon vanilla extract
- 1-2 tablespoons milk or heavy cream (as needed for consistency)

For Decoration (optional):

- Additional chopped pecans
- Shredded coconut

Instructions:

1. **Preheat Oven and Prepare Pans:**
    - Preheat your oven to 350°F (175°C).
    - Grease and flour three 8-inch round cake pans or two 9-inch round cake pans. You can also line the bottoms with parchment paper for easy removal.
2. **Mix Dry Ingredients:**

- In a large bowl, whisk together the granulated sugar, brown sugar, flour, baking powder, baking soda, salt, cinnamon, nutmeg, and allspice.
3. **Combine Wet Ingredients:**
    - In another bowl, whisk together the vegetable oil, eggs, and vanilla extract.
    - Stir in the mashed bananas, crushed pineapple, chopped pecans, and shredded coconut (if using).
4. **Combine Dry and Wet Ingredients:**
    - Gradually add the wet ingredients to the dry ingredients, stirring until just combined. Do not overmix; it's okay if there are a few lumps.
5. **Bake the Cake:**
    - Divide the batter evenly among the prepared cake pans.
    - Bake for 25-30 minutes, or until a toothpick inserted into the center of the cakes comes out clean.
    - Let the cakes cool in the pans for 10 minutes, then transfer to a wire rack to cool completely.
6. **Prepare the Cream Cheese Frosting:**
    - In a large bowl, beat the softened cream cheese and butter together until smooth and creamy.
    - Gradually add the powdered sugar, beating until well combined.
    - Stir in the vanilla extract and enough milk or heavy cream to achieve your desired consistency.
7. **Assemble and Frost the Cake:**
    - If the cakes have domed tops, level them with a knife to ensure they stack evenly.
    - Place one layer of cake on a serving plate or cake stand and spread a layer of cream cheese frosting on top.
    - Repeat with the remaining layers, and then frost the top and sides of the cake with the remaining cream cheese frosting.
8. **Decorate:**
    - Garnish the cake with additional chopped pecans and shredded coconut if desired.
9. **Serve:**
    - Slice and enjoy this moist, flavorful Hummingbird Cake with friends and family!

Hummingbird Cake is known for its incredible flavor and moist texture, making it a beloved dessert at gatherings and special occasions.

Key Lime Pie

Ingredients:

For the Graham Cracker Crust:

- 1 1/2 cups graham cracker crumbs (about 12-14 graham crackers, crushed)
- 1/4 cup granulated sugar
- 1/2 cup unsalted butter, melted

For the Key Lime Filling:

- 1 can (14 oz) sweetened condensed milk
- 1/2 cup sour cream
- 1/2 cup freshly squeezed key lime juice (about 10-12 key limes or use regular lime juice if key limes are not available)
- 3 large egg yolks
- 1 teaspoon grated lime zest (optional, for added flavor)

For the Whipped Cream Topping:

- 1 cup heavy cream
- 2 tablespoons powdered sugar
- 1 teaspoon vanilla extract

For Garnish (optional):

- Lime slices or wedges
- Additional lime zest

Instructions:

1. **Prepare the Graham Cracker Crust:**
    - Preheat your oven to 350°F (175°C).
    - In a medium bowl, combine graham cracker crumbs, granulated sugar, and melted butter. Mix until the crumbs are evenly coated and the mixture resembles wet sand.
    - Press the mixture into the bottom and up the sides of a 9-inch pie dish, using the back of a spoon or the bottom of a glass to pack it down firmly.
    - Bake the crust for 8-10 minutes, or until it's lightly golden. Remove from the oven and let cool while you prepare the filling.
2. **Prepare the Key Lime Filling:**
    - In a large bowl, whisk together the sweetened condensed milk, sour cream, key lime juice, and egg yolks until smooth and well combined.

- Stir in the grated lime zest if using.
3. **Fill and Bake the Pie:**
    - Pour the filling into the cooled graham cracker crust and smooth the top with a spatula.
    - Bake the pie in the preheated oven for 10-12 minutes, or until the filling is set but still slightly jiggly in the center.
    - Turn off the oven and let the pie cool in the oven with the door slightly ajar for 1 hour to help it set evenly.
4. **Chill:**
    - After the pie has cooled, refrigerate it for at least 3 hours or overnight to allow it to fully set and develop the flavors.
5. **Prepare the Whipped Cream Topping:**
    - In a medium bowl, use an electric mixer to beat the heavy cream until it starts to thicken.
    - Add powdered sugar and vanilla extract, then continue to beat until stiff peaks form.
6. **Serve:**
    - Spread or pipe the whipped cream over the chilled pie.
    - Garnish with lime slices or wedges and additional lime zest if desired.
7. **Enjoy:**
    - Slice and serve this tangy, creamy Key Lime Pie. It's perfect for any occasion and is sure to be a hit with anyone who enjoys a citrusy dessert!

Key Lime Pie is a timeless dessert that brings a taste of the Florida Keys to your table. Its combination of tart and sweet flavors with a buttery crust makes it a refreshing treat.

Banana Foster

Ingredients:

- 4 ripe bananas, peeled and sliced into 1/2-inch thick rounds
- 1/4 cup unsalted butter
- 1/2 cup packed brown sugar
- 1/2 teaspoon ground cinnamon
- 1/4 cup dark rum
- 1/4 cup banana liqueur (optional)
- 1 teaspoon vanilla extract
- Vanilla ice cream, for serving

Instructions:

1. **Prepare the Sauce:**
    - In a large skillet or sauté pan, melt the butter over medium heat.
2. **Add Sugar and Cinnamon:**
    - Stir in the brown sugar and ground cinnamon. Cook, stirring occasionally, until the sugar has completely dissolved and the mixture is bubbly.
3. **Add Bananas:**
    - Add the sliced bananas to the skillet. Cook for 1-2 minutes, gently stirring to coat the bananas with the sauce. Be careful not to overcook the bananas; they should be tender but still hold their shape.
4. **Flambé the Sauce (Optional):**
    - Remove the skillet from the heat and carefully add the rum. If using banana liqueur, add it at this stage.
    - Return the skillet to the heat and carefully ignite the alcohol with a long lighter. Allow the flames to subside as the alcohol burns off, which should take about 1-2 minutes. (If you prefer not to flambé, simply stir in the rum and let it heat through.)
5. **Finish the Sauce:**
    - Stir in the vanilla extract and cook for an additional minute, allowing the flavors to meld and the sauce to thicken slightly.
6. **Serve:**
    - Spoon the warm Banana Foster sauce and bananas over scoops of vanilla ice cream.
7. **Enjoy:**
    - Serve immediately while the sauce is warm and the ice cream is melting slightly.

Tips:

- **Flambéing Safety:** If you choose to flambé the sauce, be sure to exercise caution. Keep a fire extinguisher nearby and never flambé near an open flame or gas burner.
- **Banana Ripeness:** Use ripe but firm bananas. Overripe bananas may become mushy during cooking.

Banana Foster is a spectacular dessert that combines warm, caramelized bananas with creamy vanilla ice cream. It's perfect for special occasions or as an indulgent treat.

Pineapple Upside-Down Cake

Ingredients:

For the Topping:

- 1/4 cup unsalted butter
- 1 cup packed light brown sugar
- 1 can (20 oz) sliced pineapple rings in juice, drained (reserve the juice)
- Maraschino cherries (optional, for garnish)

For the Cake:

- 1 1/2 cups all-purpose flour
- 1 1/2 teaspoons baking powder
- 1/2 teaspoon salt
- 1/2 cup unsalted butter, softened
- 1 cup granulated sugar
- 2 large eggs
- 1 teaspoon vanilla extract
- 1/2 cup whole milk
- 1/2 cup pineapple juice (reserved from the pineapple can)

Instructions:

1. **Prepare the Topping:**
    - Preheat your oven to 350°F (175°C).
    - In a medium saucepan, melt 1/4 cup butter over medium heat.
    - Stir in the brown sugar and cook until the mixture is bubbly and the sugar has dissolved. Remove from heat.
2. **Assemble the Topping:**
    - Pour the brown sugar mixture into the bottom of a 9-inch round cake pan, spreading it evenly.
    - Arrange the pineapple rings over the sugar mixture. Place a maraschino cherry in the center of each pineapple ring if using.
3. **Prepare the Cake Batter:**
    - In a medium bowl, whisk together flour, baking powder, and salt.
    - In a large bowl, cream the softened butter and granulated sugar together until light and fluffy.
    - Beat in the eggs, one at a time, then stir in the vanilla extract.
    - Gradually add the flour mixture to the butter mixture, alternating with the milk and pineapple juice, beginning and ending with the flour mixture. Mix until just combined.
4. **Pour the Batter:**

- Gently pour the cake batter over the pineapple rings in the cake pan, spreading it evenly.
5. **Bake the Cake:**
    - Bake in the preheated oven for 35-40 minutes, or until a toothpick inserted into the center of the cake comes out clean and the cake is golden brown.
6. **Cool and Invert:**
    - Let the cake cool in the pan for about 10 minutes. Run a knife around the edges to loosen it.
    - Invert the cake onto a serving plate or cake stand. Tap the pan gently to release the cake and remove it.
7. **Serve:**
    - Slice and serve the cake warm or at room temperature. It's delicious on its own or with a dollop of whipped cream or a scoop of vanilla ice cream.

Tips:

- **Pan Preparation:** Ensure the cake pan is well greased and lined if necessary, to prevent sticking.
- **Pineapple Rings:** You can use fresh pineapple rings if you prefer, but canned pineapple is convenient and often used for this recipe.
- **Testing for Doneness:** Make sure the cake is fully baked by checking for a clean toothpick test and looking for a golden-brown color.

Pineapple Upside-Down Cake is a timeless dessert that's both eye-catching and delicious. The caramelized pineapple topping adds a beautiful finish and a burst of flavor that makes this cake a standout treat.

Coconut Panna Cotta

Ingredients:

For the Panna Cotta:

- 1 cup coconut milk (full-fat for a creamier texture)
- 1 cup heavy cream
- 1/2 cup granulated sugar
- 1 teaspoon vanilla extract
- 1 packet (about 2 1/4 teaspoons) unflavored gelatin powder
- 3 tablespoons cold water

For the Garnish (optional):

- Toasted coconut flakes
- Fresh fruit (e.g., mango, berries)
- A drizzle of honey or coconut sauce

Instructions:

1. **Prepare the Gelatin:**
   - In a small bowl, sprinkle the gelatin powder over 3 tablespoons of cold water. Let it sit for 5 minutes to bloom (absorb the water and swell).
2. **Heat the Coconut Milk and Cream:**
   - In a medium saucepan, combine the coconut milk, heavy cream, and granulated sugar.
   - Heat over medium heat, stirring occasionally, until the sugar is dissolved and the mixture is hot but not boiling.
3. **Dissolve the Gelatin:**
   - Remove the saucepan from the heat.
   - Stir the bloomed gelatin into the hot coconut mixture until it's completely dissolved. This may take a minute or two.
4. **Add Vanilla:**
   - Stir in the vanilla extract.
5. **Pour and Chill:**
   - Pour the mixture into individual serving glasses or molds.
   - Let the panna cotta cool to room temperature, then cover and refrigerate for at least 4 hours, or until set. The panna cotta should be firm but still slightly wobbly in the center.
6. **Garnish and Serve:**
   - Before serving, garnish with toasted coconut flakes, fresh fruit, and a drizzle of honey or coconut sauce if desired.

Tips:

- **Serving Molds:** If you use molds and want to unmold the panna cotta, lightly grease them with a neutral oil or use silicone molds for easy release.
- **Flavors:** You can infuse additional flavors by adding a small amount of shredded coconut, lime zest, or a splash of rum to the coconut milk mixture before heating.

Coconut Panna Cotta is a refined and refreshing dessert that combines the creamy texture of traditional panna cotta with the tropical flavor of coconut. It's perfect for special occasions or as a luxurious treat.

Mango Coconut Rice Pudding

Ingredients:

- 1 cup jasmine rice or short-grain rice
- 1 1/2 cups water
- 1 can (13.5 oz) coconut milk (full-fat for creaminess)
- 1 cup whole milk
- 1/2 cup granulated sugar
- 1/4 teaspoon salt
- 1/2 teaspoon vanilla extract
- 1 cup diced fresh mango (or frozen, thawed)
- 1 tablespoon cornstarch (optional, for thicker pudding)

For Garnish (optional):

- Toasted coconut flakes
- Extra diced mango
- Fresh mint leaves

Instructions:

1. **Cook the Rice:**
    - Rinse the rice under cold water until the water runs clear to remove excess starch.
    - In a medium saucepan, combine the rinsed rice and 1 1/2 cups of water. Bring to a boil over medium-high heat.
    - Reduce the heat to low, cover, and simmer for 15 minutes, or until the water is absorbed and the rice is tender.
2. **Prepare the Pudding Base:**
    - In a separate saucepan, combine the coconut milk, whole milk, sugar, and salt.
    - Heat over medium heat, stirring occasionally, until the sugar is dissolved and the mixture is hot but not boiling.
3. **Combine and Cook:**
    - Add the cooked rice to the hot milk mixture. Stir to combine.
    - Cook the mixture over medium heat, stirring frequently, for 15-20 minutes, or until the pudding has thickened to your desired consistency. If you prefer a thicker pudding, you can dissolve 1 tablespoon of cornstarch in a little water and stir it into the pudding during the last 5 minutes of cooking.
4. **Add Vanilla and Mango:**
    - Remove the saucepan from heat and stir in the vanilla extract.
    - Gently fold in the diced mango, reserving some for garnish if desired.
5. **Cool and Serve:**

- Allow the pudding to cool slightly before serving, or refrigerate it for a chilled dessert.
 - Serve in individual bowls or glasses, garnished with toasted coconut flakes, additional diced mango, and fresh mint leaves if using.

Tips:

- **Mango:** Fresh mango is preferred for its flavor and texture, but frozen mango can be used if fresh is not available. Just be sure to thaw and drain it well.
- **Consistency:** The pudding will thicken further as it cools. If it becomes too thick, stir in a little more milk or coconut milk to reach your desired consistency.

Mango Coconut Rice Pudding is a tropical twist on a classic comfort dessert, combining creamy coconut and sweet mango for a deliciously indulgent treat.

Island Coconut Cream Pie

Ingredients:

For the Pie Crust:

- 1 1/2 cups all-purpose flour
- 1/4 cup granulated sugar
- 1/2 teaspoon salt
- 1/2 cup unsalted butter, cold and cubed
- 1/4 cup ice water (more if needed)

For the Coconut Cream Filling:

- 1 cup whole milk
- 1 cup coconut milk (full-fat)
- 1 cup granulated sugar
- 1/4 cup cornstarch
- 1/4 teaspoon salt
- 4 large egg yolks
- 2 tablespoons unsalted butter
- 1 teaspoon vanilla extract
- 1 cup shredded sweetened coconut (toasted or untoasted)

For the Whipped Cream Topping:

- 1 cup heavy cream
- 2 tablespoons powdered sugar
- 1 teaspoon vanilla extract
- 1/2 cup toasted shredded coconut (for garnish)

Instructions:

1. **Prepare the Pie Crust:**
    - In a large bowl, whisk together the flour, sugar, and salt.
    - Cut in the cold butter using a pastry cutter or your fingers until the mixture resembles coarse crumbs.
    - Gradually add the ice water, a tablespoon at a time, until the dough comes together. Avoid overworking the dough.
    - Form the dough into a disk, wrap it in plastic wrap, and refrigerate for at least 30 minutes.
2. **Preheat Oven and Prepare Crust:**
    - Preheat your oven to 375°F (190°C).
    - On a lightly floured surface, roll out the dough to fit a 9-inch pie dish. Press the dough into the dish and trim any excess.
    - Prick the bottom of the crust with a fork to prevent bubbling.
    - Line the crust with parchment paper and fill with pie weights or dried beans.

- Bake for 15 minutes, then remove the weights and parchment paper and bake for an additional 5-7 minutes, or until the crust is golden brown. Let it cool completely.

3. **Prepare the Coconut Cream Filling:**
   - In a medium saucepan, whisk together the milk, coconut milk, sugar, cornstarch, and salt. Cook over medium heat, whisking constantly, until the mixture starts to thicken and bubble.
   - In a small bowl, whisk the egg yolks. Gradually add a small amount of the hot milk mixture to the egg yolks to temper them, then whisk the egg yolks back into the saucepan.
   - Continue to cook the mixture, whisking constantly, until it becomes thick and coats the back of a spoon.
   - Remove from heat and stir in the butter, vanilla extract, and shredded coconut.
   - Pour the filling into the cooled pie crust and smooth the top with a spatula. Cover with plastic wrap and refrigerate for at least 4 hours or until fully set.

4. **Prepare the Whipped Cream Topping:**
   - In a large bowl, beat the heavy cream, powdered sugar, and vanilla extract with an electric mixer until stiff peaks form.

5. **Assemble and Garnish:**
   - Spread the whipped cream over the chilled pie.
   - Garnish with toasted shredded coconut.

6. **Serve:**
   - Slice and serve the pie chilled. Enjoy the creamy, tropical flavors of this indulgent dessert!

Tips:

- **Toasting Coconut:** To toast shredded coconut, spread it in a single layer on a baking sheet and bake at 350°F (175°C) for 5-7 minutes, stirring occasionally until golden brown.
- **Chilling:** Make sure the pie is well-chilled before serving to ensure the filling is fully set and the whipped cream topping holds its shape.

Island Coconut Cream Pie is a delightful treat that brings a taste of the tropics to your dessert table. Its rich coconut custard and creamy topping make it a perfect choice for any special occasion or a delicious everyday indulgence.

Jamaican Jerk Brownies

Ingredients:

For the Brownies:

- 1 cup (2 sticks) unsalted butter
- 1 cup granulated sugar
- 1 cup packed brown sugar
- 4 large eggs
- 1 teaspoon vanilla extract
- 1 cup all-purpose flour
- 1 cup unsweetened cocoa powder
- 1/2 teaspoon salt
- 1/2 teaspoon baking powder
- 1-2 teaspoons Jamaican jerk seasoning (adjust to taste, see note for homemade version)

For the Jerk Chocolate Ganache (optional):

- 1 cup semisweet chocolate chips
- 1/2 cup heavy cream
- 1/2 teaspoon Jamaican jerk seasoning (adjust to taste)

For Garnish (optional):

- Extra jerk seasoning
- Fresh mint leaves or a sprinkle of sea salt

Instructions:

1. **Preheat Oven:**
    - Preheat your oven to 350°F (175°C).
    - Line a 9x13-inch baking pan with parchment paper, leaving some overhang for easy removal, or lightly grease the pan.
2. **Prepare the Brownie Batter:**
    - In a medium saucepan, melt the butter over low heat. Remove from heat and stir in the granulated sugar and brown sugar until well combined.
    - Beat in the eggs, one at a time, then stir in the vanilla extract.
    - In a separate bowl, whisk together the flour, cocoa powder, salt, and baking powder.
    - Gradually add the dry ingredients to the wet ingredients, stirring until just combined.

- Fold in the Jamaican jerk seasoning, starting with 1 teaspoon and adjusting to taste. Be cautious, as jerk seasoning can be quite spicy.

3. **Bake the Brownies:**
    - Pour the batter into the prepared baking pan and spread it evenly.
    - Bake for 25-30 minutes, or until a toothpick inserted into the center comes out with a few moist crumbs. The edges should be set but the center slightly fudgy.
    - Allow the brownies to cool in the pan on a wire rack before cutting into squares.
4. **Prepare the Jerk Chocolate Ganache (Optional):**
    - In a small saucepan, heat the heavy cream over medium heat until it begins to simmer. Remove from heat.
    - Add the chocolate chips and let them sit for 1-2 minutes, then stir until smooth and glossy.
    - Stir in the jerk seasoning to taste.
    - Pour or drizzle the ganache over the cooled brownies.
5. **Garnish and Serve:**
    - If desired, sprinkle extra jerk seasoning over the brownies or add a pinch of sea salt for extra flavor.
    - Garnish with fresh mint leaves if desired.
6. **Enjoy:**
    - Slice and serve the brownies. They can be enjoyed as is or with a scoop of vanilla ice cream for an extra treat.

Tips:

- **Adjusting Spice Level:** Jamaican jerk seasoning can be quite spicy. Start with a small amount and taste the batter to adjust the heat level to your preference.
- **Homemade Jerk Seasoning:** If you prefer homemade jerk seasoning, combine spices like allspice, thyme, cinnamon, nutmeg, garlic powder, onion powder, paprika, cayenne pepper, and salt. Adjust quantities to taste.

Jamaican Jerk Brownies offer a delicious twist on traditional brownies, combining the rich flavors of chocolate with the complex, spicy notes of jerk seasoning. This fusion dessert is sure to be a hit for those who enjoy a little heat with their sweet!

Guava Cheesecake

Ingredients:

For the Graham Cracker Crust:

- 1 1/2 cups graham cracker crumbs (about 12-14 graham crackers, crushed)
- 1/4 cup granulated sugar
- 1/2 cup unsalted butter, melted

For the Cheesecake Filling:

- 4 (8 oz) packages cream cheese, softened
- 1 cup granulated sugar
- 1 teaspoon vanilla extract
- 4 large eggs
- 1 cup sour cream
- 1 cup guava paste or guava puree (see note for guava paste preparation)

For the Guava Glaze (Optional):

- 1/2 cup guava juice or guava puree
- 2 tablespoons granulated sugar
- 1 tablespoon cornstarch
- 1 tablespoon water

For Garnish (Optional):

- Fresh guava slices
- Whipped cream
- Mint leaves

Instructions:

1. **Prepare the Graham Cracker Crust:**
    - Preheat your oven to 350°F (175°C).
    - In a medium bowl, combine graham cracker crumbs, granulated sugar, and melted butter. Mix until the crumbs are evenly coated and the mixture resembles wet sand.
    - Press the mixture firmly into the bottom of a 9-inch springform pan to form an even layer.
    - Bake for 8-10 minutes, or until the crust is lightly golden. Remove from the oven and let cool while you prepare the filling.
2. **Prepare the Cheesecake Filling:**

- In a large mixing bowl, beat the softened cream cheese until smooth and creamy.
- Gradually add the sugar and continue to beat until well combined.
- Add the vanilla extract and beat until incorporated.
- Beat in the eggs, one at a time, making sure each egg is fully incorporated before adding the next.
- Mix in the sour cream until smooth.
- Gently fold in the guava paste or guava puree. If using guava paste, ensure it is softened slightly for easier mixing.

3. **Bake the Cheesecake:**
    - Pour the cheesecake filling over the cooled graham cracker crust, smoothing the top with a spatula.
    - Bake in the preheated oven for 55-65 minutes, or until the center is set and the edges are slightly puffed. The center should still have a slight jiggle.
    - Turn off the oven and let the cheesecake cool in the oven with the door slightly ajar for 1 hour. This helps prevent cracking.
4. **Chill:**
    - After the cheesecake has cooled, refrigerate it for at least 4 hours or overnight to allow it to set completely.
5. **Prepare the Guava Glaze (Optional):**
    - In a small saucepan, combine guava juice or puree, granulated sugar, cornstarch, and water.
    - Heat over medium heat, stirring constantly, until the mixture thickens and becomes translucent.
    - Remove from heat and let it cool before spreading over the chilled cheesecake.
6. **Garnish and Serve:**
    - Once the cheesecake is chilled, spread or drizzle the guava glaze over the top, if using.
    - Garnish with fresh guava slices, whipped cream, and mint leaves, if desired.
7. **Enjoy:**
    - Slice and serve your delicious Guava Cheesecake. It's a tropical treat that's perfect for any special occasion or as a unique dessert for a regular meal.

Tips:

- **Guava Paste Preparation:** If using guava paste, cut it into small pieces and microwave for a few seconds to soften it before mixing into the cheesecake batter.
- **Avoid Cracking:** To minimize cracks, avoid overmixing the batter and ensure the cheesecake cools slowly in the oven.

Guava Cheesecake brings a tropical flair to a beloved dessert, combining the creamy richness of cheesecake with the sweet and exotic flavor of guava. It's a perfect choice for those who want to enjoy a unique and delicious treat.

Papaya Lime Parfait

Ingredients:

For the Papaya Layer:

- 2 ripe papayas, peeled, seeded, and diced
- 2 tablespoons honey or agave syrup (optional, depending on the sweetness of the papaya)
- Juice of 1 lime

For the Yogurt Layer:

- 2 cups Greek yogurt (plain or vanilla)
- 2 tablespoons honey or maple syrup
- Zest of 1 lime

For Assembly:

- Granola (store-bought or homemade)
- Fresh mint leaves (for garnish, optional)
- Lime wedges (for garnish, optional)

Instructions:

1. **Prepare the Papaya Layer:**
   - In a medium bowl, combine the diced papaya, honey (if using), and lime juice. Gently toss to coat the papaya evenly. Set aside.
2. **Prepare the Yogurt Layer:**
   - In a separate bowl, mix the Greek yogurt with honey or maple syrup and lime zest. Stir until well combined.
3. **Assemble the Parfaits:**
   - In serving glasses or bowls, start by spooning a layer of the lime yogurt at the bottom.
   - Add a layer of the papaya mixture on top of the yogurt.
   - Repeat the layers until the glasses or bowls are filled, finishing with a layer of papaya on top.
4. **Add Granola:**
   - Sprinkle granola over the top layer of papaya just before serving to maintain its crunch.
5. **Garnish and Serve:**
   - Garnish with fresh mint leaves and lime wedges if desired.
   - Serve immediately for the best texture or refrigerate until ready to serve.

Tips:

- **Papaya Ripeness:** Choose ripe papayas for the best flavor. They should be slightly soft to the touch but not mushy.
- **Yogurt Alternatives:** If you prefer a dairy-free option, you can use coconut or almond milk yogurt.
- **Granola:** Use your favorite granola or make your own by toasting oats, nuts, and seeds with a little honey or maple syrup.

Papaya Lime Parfait is a vibrant and nutritious dessert that combines tropical flavors with creamy yogurt and crunchy granola. It's a great way to enjoy fresh fruit and is perfect for a light breakfast, a healthy snack, or a delightful dessert.

Taro Root Cake

Ingredients:

For the Cake:

- 1 lb taro root, peeled and cubed
- 1 cup granulated sugar
- 1/2 cup unsalted butter, softened
- 3 large eggs
- 1 cup all-purpose flour
- 1 teaspoon baking powder
- 1/4 teaspoon salt
- 1/2 cup milk
- 1 teaspoon vanilla extract
- Optional: 1/4 cup coconut flakes or shredded coconut for added flavor

For the Taro Glaze (optional):

- 1/2 cup taro root, peeled and cubed
- 1/4 cup granulated sugar
- 1/4 cup water

For Garnish (optional):

- Whipped cream
- Fresh fruit
- Extra coconut flakes

Instructions:

1. **Prepare the Taro:**
    - Steam or boil the taro root until tender, about 15-20 minutes. Once cooked, let it cool slightly.
    - Mash the taro root until smooth. You should have about 1 cup of mashed taro.
2. **Preheat Oven and Prepare Pan:**
    - Preheat your oven to 350°F (175°C).
    - Grease and flour an 8-inch round cake pan or line it with parchment paper.
3. **Prepare the Cake Batter:**
    - In a large mixing bowl, cream together the softened butter and granulated sugar until light and fluffy.
    - Beat in the eggs, one at a time, ensuring each is fully incorporated before adding the next.
    - Mix in the mashed taro and vanilla extract.

- In a separate bowl, whisk together the flour, baking powder, and salt.
- Gradually add the dry ingredients to the wet ingredients, alternating with the milk, beginning and ending with the flour mixture. Mix until just combined.
- If using, fold in the coconut flakes.

4. **Bake the Cake:**
   - Pour the batter into the prepared cake pan and smooth the top with a spatula.
   - Bake for 30-35 minutes, or until a toothpick inserted into the center comes out clean.
   - Allow the cake to cool in the pan for 10 minutes, then transfer to a wire rack to cool completely.

5. **Prepare the Taro Glaze (Optional):**
   - In a small saucepan, combine 1/2 cup of cubed taro root, granulated sugar, and water.
   - Cook over medium heat, stirring occasionally, until the taro is soft and the mixture has thickened into a syrupy consistency. Let it cool slightly before using.
   - Drizzle the glaze over the cooled cake before serving.

6. **Garnish and Serve:**
   - Optionally, top with whipped cream, fresh fruit, or extra coconut flakes.
   - Slice and serve the taro root cake. It pairs wonderfully with a cup of tea or coffee.

Tips:

- **Taro Preparation:** Ensure the taro root is fully cooked and mashed smoothly for the best texture in the cake.
- **Flavor Variations:** For a different twist, you can add a bit of almond extract or a handful of chopped nuts to the batter.

Taro Root Cake is a unique and delicious dessert that showcases the distinctive flavor of taro. Its moist texture and subtle sweetness make it a standout treat for special occasions or a delightful addition to your regular dessert rotation.

Sweet Plantain Fritters

Ingredients:

- 3 ripe plantains (overripe for extra sweetness, but not too soft)
- 1 large egg
- 1/4 cup all-purpose flour (or more as needed)
- 2 tablespoons granulated sugar
- 1/2 teaspoon ground cinnamon
- 1/4 teaspoon salt
- 1/4 teaspoon baking powder
- 1/4 teaspoon vanilla extract (optional)
- 2 tablespoons milk (or plant-based milk)
- Vegetable oil for frying

Instructions:

1. **Prepare the Plantains:**
   - Peel the plantains and cut them into chunks.
   - In a bowl or food processor, mash the plantains until smooth. You can leave some small chunks for texture if you prefer.
2. **Mix the Batter:**
   - In a large mixing bowl, combine the mashed plantains, egg, granulated sugar, ground cinnamon, salt, baking powder, and vanilla extract (if using).
   - Gradually stir in the flour until the mixture forms a thick batter. If the batter is too thick, add a little milk to reach a spoonable consistency.
3. **Heat the Oil:**
   - Heat about 1/2 inch of vegetable oil in a large skillet over medium heat. The oil is ready when a small drop of batter sizzles upon contact.
4. **Fry the Fritters:**
   - Drop spoonfuls of the batter into the hot oil, flattening them slightly with the back of the spoon to form small patties.
   - Fry for 2-3 minutes on each side, or until golden brown and crispy. Avoid overcrowding the pan; work in batches if necessary.
5. **Drain and Serve:**
   - Remove the fritters from the oil using a slotted spoon and place them on a plate lined with paper towels to drain excess oil.
   - Serve warm, sprinkled with a little extra cinnamon sugar if desired, or with a drizzle of honey or maple syrup.
6. **Optional Garnishes:**
   - Garnish with a dusting of powdered sugar, fresh fruit, or a dollop of yogurt for added flavor and presentation.

Tips:

- **Plantain Ripeness:** Use overripe plantains for the sweetest and most flavorful fritters. They should be yellow with dark spots, but still firm enough to hold their shape.
- **Oil Temperature:** Maintain medium heat to ensure the fritters cook evenly and become crispy without burning. If the oil is too hot, the fritters might cook too quickly on the outside while remaining raw on the inside.

Sweet Plantain Fritters are a versatile and tasty treat that bring a touch of tropical flavor to your table. Their natural sweetness and crispy texture make them a delightful addition to any meal or a satisfying snack.

Caribbean Pineapple Flan

Ingredients:

For the Caramel:

- 1 cup granulated sugar
- 1/4 cup water

For the Flan:

- 1 can (14 oz) sweetened condensed milk
- 1 can (12 oz) evaporated milk
- 1 cup whole milk
- 4 large eggs
- 1 cup pineapple juice (fresh or canned)
- 1/2 cup granulated sugar
- 1 teaspoon vanilla extract
- 1/2 teaspoon ground cinnamon (optional)

For Garnish (optional):

- Pineapple slices
- Fresh mint leaves
- Whipped cream

Instructions:

1. **Prepare the Caramel:**
   - In a medium saucepan over medium heat, combine the granulated sugar and water.
   - Cook, stirring constantly, until the sugar dissolves and the mixture turns a deep amber color. Be careful not to burn it.
   - Quickly pour the caramel into the bottom of a 9-inch round baking dish or flan mold, tilting the dish to evenly coat the bottom. Set aside to cool and harden.
2. **Prepare the Flan Mixture:**
   - Preheat your oven to 350°F (175°C).
   - In a large mixing bowl, whisk together the sweetened condensed milk, evaporated milk, and whole milk.
   - Add the eggs, pineapple juice, granulated sugar, vanilla extract, and ground cinnamon (if using). Whisk until well combined and smooth.
3. **Bake the Flan:**
   - Pour the flan mixture over the hardened caramel in the baking dish.

- Place the baking dish in a larger roasting pan and carefully add hot water to the roasting pan, creating a water bath. The water should come halfway up the sides of the flan dish.
- Bake for 50-60 minutes, or until the flan is set and a knife inserted into the center comes out clean. The flan should have a slight jiggle in the center.

4. **Cool and Chill:**
   - Remove the flan from the oven and water bath, and let it cool to room temperature.
   - Cover and refrigerate for at least 4 hours or overnight to allow it to fully set.

5. **Unmold and Serve:**
   - To unmold the flan, run a knife around the edges of the flan to loosen it.
   - Place a serving plate over the top of the flan dish and carefully invert it to release the flan onto the plate.
   - Garnish with pineapple slices, fresh mint leaves, and a dollop of whipped cream, if desired.

6. **Enjoy:**
   - Slice and serve the Caribbean Pineapple Flan chilled. It's a creamy and tropical treat that's sure to impress!

Tips:

- **Caramel Preparation:** Be cautious when making caramel as it can get very hot. Don't stir once the sugar starts to melt to avoid crystallization.
- **Pineapple Juice:** For a more intense pineapple flavor, you can use fresh pineapple juice. If using canned pineapple juice, choose a 100% juice product.

Caribbean Pineapple Flan is a delightful dessert that brings a touch of tropical paradise to your table with its creamy texture and sweet pineapple flavor. It's perfect for any special occasion or as a refreshing end to a summer meal.

Rum-Soaked Banana Bread

Ingredients:

For the Banana Bread:

- 1/2 cup (1 stick) unsalted butter, softened
- 1 cup granulated sugar
- 2 large eggs
- 4 ripe bananas, mashed (about 1 1/2 cups)
- 1/4 cup milk
- 1 teaspoon vanilla extract
- 1 1/2 cups all-purpose flour
- 1 teaspoon baking powder
- 1/2 teaspoon baking soda
- 1/4 teaspoon salt
- 1/2 teaspoon ground cinnamon (optional)
- 1/2 cup chopped walnuts or pecans (optional)

For the Rum Soak:

- 1/4 cup dark rum
- 1/4 cup granulated sugar

For Garnish (optional):

- Powdered sugar
- Extra chopped nuts

Instructions:

1. **Preheat Oven and Prepare Pan:**
   - Preheat your oven to 350°F (175°C).
   - Grease and flour a 9x5-inch loaf pan or line it with parchment paper.
2. **Prepare the Banana Bread Batter:**
   - In a large bowl, cream together the softened butter and granulated sugar until light and fluffy.
   - Beat in the eggs, one at a time, ensuring each is fully incorporated before adding the next.
   - Mix in the mashed bananas, milk, and vanilla extract until well combined.
   - In a separate bowl, whisk together the flour, baking powder, baking soda, salt, and ground cinnamon (if using).
   - Gradually add the dry ingredients to the wet ingredients, mixing until just combined.

- Fold in the chopped walnuts or pecans if using.
3. **Bake the Banana Bread:**
    - Pour the batter into the prepared loaf pan and smooth the top with a spatula.
    - Bake for 60-70 minutes, or until a toothpick inserted into the center comes out clean. The top should be golden brown.
    - Allow the banana bread to cool in the pan for 10 minutes, then transfer it to a wire rack to cool completely.
4. **Prepare the Rum Soak:**
    - While the bread is cooling, in a small saucepan over medium heat, combine the dark rum and granulated sugar.
    - Stir until the sugar is completely dissolved and the mixture is heated through. Do not let it boil.
    - Remove from heat and let it cool slightly.
5. **Soak the Banana Bread:**
    - Once the banana bread is completely cooled, use a toothpick or skewer to poke holes all over the top of the bread.
    - Slowly brush or drizzle the rum mixture over the top of the bread, allowing it to soak in. You can use a pastry brush for this step.
6. **Garnish and Serve:**
    - Optionally, dust the top with powdered sugar and sprinkle with extra chopped nuts for added texture and flavor.
    - Slice and serve. This bread is great on its own or with a dollop of whipped cream or a scoop of vanilla ice cream.

Tips:

- **Ripeness of Bananas:** Use very ripe bananas for the best flavor and sweetness. They should be heavily speckled or even black.
- **Rum Choice:** Dark rum adds a rich, deep flavor, but you can also use spiced rum for extra complexity or light rum for a milder taste.

Rum-Soaked Banana Bread is a delightful dessert that combines the familiar comfort of banana bread with the sophisticated warmth of rum. It's perfect for a special occasion or as a treat to enjoy with your afternoon tea or coffee.

Passion Fruit Pavlova

Ingredients:

For the Meringue:

- 4 large egg whites (room temperature)
- 1 cup granulated sugar
- 1/4 teaspoon cream of tartar
- 1 teaspoon cornstarch
- 1 teaspoon vanilla extract
- 1 tablespoon lemon juice

For the Topping:

- 1 cup heavy cream
- 2 tablespoons powdered sugar
- 1 teaspoon vanilla extract
- 1/2 cup passion fruit pulp (fresh or from a can)
- Fresh fruit for garnish (e.g., kiwi slices, berries, or extra passion fruit pulp)

Instructions:

1. **Preheat Oven:**
    - Preheat your oven to 275°F (135°C).
    - Line a baking sheet with parchment paper and draw a 9-inch circle on the parchment as a guide for shaping the meringue.
2. **Prepare the Meringue:**
    - In a large, clean mixing bowl, beat the egg whites with an electric mixer on medium speed until foamy.
    - Add the cream of tartar and continue to beat until soft peaks form.
    - Gradually add the granulated sugar, 1 tablespoon at a time, while beating on high speed. Continue to beat until the mixture is glossy and stiff peaks form.
    - Gently fold in the cornstarch, vanilla extract, and lemon juice until well combined.
3. **Shape and Bake the Meringue:**
    - Spoon the meringue onto the parchment paper within the drawn circle, spreading it out to form a circular base with slightly raised edges to hold the toppings.
    - Use a spatula to smooth the top and create swirls or peaks for added texture.
    - Bake in the preheated oven for 1 hour and 15 minutes, or until the meringue is crisp and dry to the touch. It should be slightly golden around the edges.
    - Turn off the oven and let the meringue cool completely in the oven with the door slightly ajar. This helps prevent cracks.
4. **Prepare the Topping:**

- In a medium bowl, whip the heavy cream with an electric mixer until soft peaks form.
- Add the powdered sugar and vanilla extract, and continue to whip until stiff peaks form.

5. **Assemble the Pavlova:**
   - Once the meringue is completely cooled, carefully transfer it to a serving plate.
   - Spread the whipped cream over the meringue base, smoothing it out to cover the surface.
   - Spoon the passion fruit pulp over the top of the whipped cream. You can also add fresh fruit for extra color and flavor.
6. **Serve:**
   - Slice and serve the Passion Fruit Pavlova immediately for the best texture. It's best enjoyed fresh as the meringue can start to soften over time.

Tips:

- **Egg Whites:** Ensure your mixing bowl and beaters are completely clean and free from any grease. This helps the egg whites whip up properly.
- **Meringue Cracks:** If your meringue cracks during baking, don't worry—this can be covered with whipped cream and fruit.

Passion Fruit Pavlova is a beautiful and delicious dessert that combines the lightness of meringue with the creamy richness of whipped cream and the tangy brightness of passion fruit. It's a delightful choice for any special occasion or a sweet end to a meal.

Mango Chia Seed Pudding

Ingredients:

- 1/2 cup chia seeds
- 2 cups coconut milk (or any milk of your choice, such as almond, soy, or dairy milk)
- 1/4 cup pure maple syrup or honey (adjust to taste)
- 1 teaspoon vanilla extract
- 1 1/2 cups ripe mango, peeled and diced (fresh or frozen)
- Optional toppings: shredded coconut, fresh mint leaves, additional diced mango

Instructions:

1. **Prepare the Chia Seed Mixture:**
    - In a large bowl or a jar with a lid, combine the chia seeds, coconut milk, maple syrup (or honey), and vanilla extract.
    - Stir well to ensure the chia seeds are evenly distributed and not clumping together.
    - Cover and refrigerate for at least 4 hours or overnight. The chia seeds will absorb the liquid and form a thick, pudding-like consistency.
2. **Prepare the Mango Puree:**
    - While the chia pudding is setting, prepare the mango puree. If using fresh mango, peel and dice the mango, then blend it in a food processor or blender until smooth.
    - If using frozen mango, thaw it slightly before blending.
    - Optionally, you can mix a bit of maple syrup or honey into the mango puree for extra sweetness.
3. **Assemble the Pudding:**
    - Once the chia pudding has set and thickened, gently stir it to ensure an even consistency.
    - Spoon the chia pudding into serving bowls or jars.
4. **Add Mango Puree:**
    - Top each serving of chia pudding with a layer of mango puree. You can swirl the puree into the pudding or leave it as a separate layer.
5. **Garnish and Serve:**
    - Garnish with optional toppings like shredded coconut, fresh mint leaves, or additional diced mango for added texture and flavor.
    - Serve chilled and enjoy!

Tips:

- **Chia Seeds:** Make sure to stir the chia seed mixture well right after combining the ingredients to prevent clumping. You can also stir it once or twice during the initial setting period if you like.
- **Adjusting Sweetness:** Taste the mango puree and adjust the sweetness if needed before adding it to the chia pudding.
- **Make-Ahead:** This pudding is perfect for meal prep. You can make it up to 3 days in advance and store it in the refrigerator.

Mango Chia Seed Pudding is a deliciously healthy dessert that's naturally sweet and rich in nutrients. It's a great option for breakfast, a snack, or a light dessert, and the tropical flavor makes it a refreshing treat for any time of year.

Coconut Pineapple Muffins

Ingredients:

- 1 1/2 cups all-purpose flour
- 1/2 cup shredded coconut (unsweetened or sweetened, as preferred)
- 1/2 cup granulated sugar
- 1/4 cup brown sugar
- 2 teaspoons baking powder
- 1/2 teaspoon baking soda
- 1/4 teaspoon salt
- 1/2 cup unsalted butter, melted and cooled
- 2 large eggs
- 1/2 cup milk (dairy or non-dairy)
- 1 teaspoon vanilla extract
- 1 cup crushed pineapple, drained
- Optional: 1/2 cup chopped nuts (e.g., macadamia nuts or pecans)

Instructions:

1. **Preheat Oven and Prepare Pan:**
   - Preheat your oven to 375°F (190°C).
   - Line a 12-cup muffin tin with paper liners or lightly grease it.
2. **Prepare the Dry Ingredients:**
   - In a large bowl, whisk together the flour, shredded coconut, granulated sugar, brown sugar, baking powder, baking soda, and salt.
3. **Prepare the Wet Ingredients:**
   - In a separate bowl, whisk together the melted butter, eggs, milk, and vanilla extract until well combined.
4. **Combine Ingredients:**
   - Add the wet ingredients to the dry ingredients and stir gently until just combined. Be careful not to overmix; the batter should be lumpy.
   - Fold in the crushed pineapple and chopped nuts, if using.
5. **Fill Muffin Tin:**
   - Divide the batter evenly among the 12 muffin cups, filling each about 2/3 full.
6. **Bake:**
   - Bake in the preheated oven for 18-22 minutes, or until the tops are golden brown and a toothpick inserted into the center of a muffin comes out clean.
7. **Cool and Serve:**
   - Allow the muffins to cool in the pan for 5 minutes before transferring them to a wire rack to cool completely.
8. **Enjoy:**

- Serve warm or at room temperature. These muffins are delightful on their own or with a touch of butter.

Tips:

- **Draining Pineapple:** Make sure to drain the pineapple well to avoid adding excess moisture to the batter. You can use a fine mesh sieve or press it between paper towels to remove excess liquid.
- **Coconut:** If you prefer a more intense coconut flavor, you can use toasted shredded coconut or increase the amount of coconut used in the recipe.

Coconut Pineapple Muffins are a delightful treat that brings a taste of the tropics to your kitchen. They're perfect for starting your day with a burst of flavor or for enjoying with a cup of tea or coffee.

Tropical Trifle

Ingredients:

For the Fruit Layer:

- 1 can (20 oz) pineapple chunks, drained
- 1 1/2 cups mango, peeled and diced (fresh or frozen)
- 1 cup strawberries, hulled and sliced (or use other tropical fruits like kiwi or passion fruit)

For the Cake Layer:

- 1 pound cake or sponge cake, cut into cubes (store-bought or homemade)
- Optional: 1/4 cup coconut rum or fruit juice (for soaking)

For the Cream Layer:

- 2 cups heavy cream
- 1/4 cup powdered sugar
- 1 teaspoon vanilla extract
- 1/2 cup coconut cream or coconut yogurt (optional, for added coconut flavor)

For Garnish:

- Shredded coconut
- Fresh mint leaves
- Additional fruit slices (mango, pineapple, strawberries)

Instructions:

1. **Prepare the Cream Layer:**
    - In a large mixing bowl, whip the heavy cream with an electric mixer until it starts to thicken.
    - Add the powdered sugar and vanilla extract, and continue to whip until stiff peaks form.
    - If using coconut cream or yogurt, gently fold it into the whipped cream for added coconut flavor.
2. **Prepare the Fruit Layer:**
    - In a bowl, combine the pineapple chunks, diced mango, and sliced strawberries. Set aside.
3. **Prepare the Cake Layer:**
    - If desired, lightly soak the cake cubes in coconut rum or fruit juice for extra flavor and moisture.
    - Arrange the cake cubes as the first layer in your trifle dish.

4. **Assemble the Trifle:**
    - Spread a layer of the fruit mixture over the cake cubes.
    - Spoon or pipe a layer of the whipped cream over the fruit.
    - Repeat the layers (cake, fruit, and cream) until you reach the top of the dish, ending with a layer of whipped cream.
5. **Garnish:**
    - Sprinkle shredded coconut over the top layer of whipped cream.
    - Garnish with fresh mint leaves and additional fruit slices for a beautiful presentation.
6. **Chill:**
    - Refrigerate the trifle for at least 2 hours, or preferably overnight, to allow the flavors to meld and the layers to set.
7. **Serve:**
    - Serve chilled, scooping out portions of the trifle to showcase the beautiful layers.

Tips:

- **Cake Alternatives:** If you prefer, you can use ladyfingers, shortbread cookies, or even brownies in place of the pound cake.
- **Fruit Variations:** Feel free to customize the fruit layers based on what's in season or your personal preferences. Tropical fruits like kiwi, passion fruit, or papaya work well.

Tropical Trifle is a delightful dessert that brings together the vibrant flavors of the tropics in a visually appealing way. It's perfect for special occasions, holiday gatherings, or any time you want to enjoy a refreshing and indulgent treat.

Caramelized Banana Tarte Tatin

Ingredients:

For the Caramel:

- 1 cup granulated sugar
- 1/4 cup water
- 1/4 cup unsalted butter (cut into pieces)

For the Banana Layer:

- 4-5 ripe bananas, peeled and halved lengthwise
- 2 tablespoons unsalted butter
- 1/4 cup brown sugar

For the Pastry:

- 1 sheet of puff pastry (thawed if frozen)
- Optional: 1 egg (for egg wash)
- Optional: 1 tablespoon granulated sugar (for sprinkling)

Instructions:

1. **Preheat Oven:**
   - Preheat your oven to 375°F (190°C).
2. **Prepare the Caramel:**
   - In a medium saucepan over medium heat, combine the granulated sugar and water.
   - Cook, without stirring, until the sugar dissolves and the mixture turns a deep amber color. Swirl the pan gently if needed to ensure even caramelization.
   - Remove from heat and carefully stir in the butter until smooth and combined. Be cautious as the mixture may bubble vigorously.
3. **Prepare the Banana Layer:**
   - In a skillet, melt the 2 tablespoons of butter over medium heat.
   - Add the brown sugar and stir until it dissolves and starts to bubble.
   - Place the banana halves in the skillet cut-side down and cook for 2-3 minutes until they start to caramelize. Turn the bananas over and cook for an additional 2 minutes. Remove from heat.
4. **Assemble the Tarte Tatin:**
   - Pour the caramel into a 9-inch (23 cm) ovenproof skillet or a round baking dish.
   - Arrange the caramelized banana halves in a circular pattern over the caramel, cut-side down.
5. **Top with Pastry:**

- Roll out the puff pastry slightly if needed to fit the skillet or dish. Drape the pastry over the bananas, tucking the edges down around the sides of the skillet.
- If using, beat the egg and brush it over the pastry for a golden finish. Sprinkle granulated sugar on top of the pastry for extra sweetness and crunch.

6. **Bake:**
   - Bake in the preheated oven for 20-25 minutes, or until the pastry is golden brown and puffed.
7. **Invert and Serve:**
   - Allow the tarte tatin to cool for 5 minutes. Carefully invert it onto a serving plate, so the bananas are on top. Be cautious of hot caramel.
   - Serve warm or at room temperature. It's delightful on its own or with a dollop of whipped cream or a scoop of vanilla ice cream.

Tips:

- **Caramel Temperature:** Be careful with the caramel, as it can get very hot and may burn if overcooked. Remove it from the heat as soon as it reaches the desired color.
- **Banana Ripeness:** Use ripe but firm bananas to avoid them becoming too mushy during baking.
- **Pastry Alternatives:** If you prefer, you can use a homemade pie crust or a pre-made pie dough instead of puff pastry.

Caramelized Banana Tarte Tatin is a luxurious and comforting dessert that combines the rich flavors of caramel with the sweet, buttery goodness of bananas. It's a wonderful way to end a meal or to impress guests with a unique and delicious treat.

Pineapple and Coconut Smoothie Bowl

Ingredients:

For the Smoothie:

- 1 cup frozen pineapple chunks
- 1/2 cup frozen banana slices
- 1/2 cup coconut milk (or any milk of your choice)
- 1/4 cup Greek yogurt (optional, for added creaminess)
- 1 tablespoon honey or maple syrup (optional, for added sweetness)
- 1 tablespoon shredded coconut (optional, for extra coconut flavor)

For the Toppings:

- Fresh pineapple slices or chunks
- Sliced banana
- Granola
- Chia seeds
- Shredded coconut
- Fresh mint leaves
- Optional: berries (such as strawberries, blueberries), nuts, or seeds

Instructions:

1. **Prepare the Smoothie:**
   - In a blender, combine the frozen pineapple chunks, frozen banana slices, coconut milk, Greek yogurt (if using), and honey or maple syrup (if desired). Add the shredded coconut if you want an extra coconut flavor.
   - Blend until smooth and creamy. If the mixture is too thick, add a little more coconut milk to reach your desired consistency.
2. **Assemble the Smoothie Bowl:**
   - Pour the smoothie into a bowl, smoothing the top with the back of a spoon.
3. **Add Toppings:**
   - Arrange your desired toppings on top of the smoothie in an attractive pattern. Be creative with your arrangement to make it visually appealing.
   - For example, you might place fresh pineapple chunks and banana slices in a circular pattern, sprinkle granola in one section, and scatter chia seeds and shredded coconut over the top.
4. **Serve:**
   - Serve immediately for the best texture and freshness.

Tips:

- **Texture:** If you prefer a thicker smoothie bowl, use more frozen fruit and less liquid. For a thinner consistency, add more coconut milk.

- **Customization:** Feel free to customize the toppings based on your preferences and what you have on hand. Fresh fruits, nuts, seeds, and granola are all great choices.
- **Sweetness:** Adjust the sweetness according to your taste. If the smoothie is not sweet enough, add a bit more honey or maple syrup.

Pineapple and Coconut Smoothie Bowl is not only delicious but also packed with vitamins and nutrients. It's a tropical escape in a bowl that can be enjoyed any time of day.

Island Spice Cupcakes

Ingredients:

For the Cupcakes:

- 1 1/2 cups all-purpose flour
- 1 teaspoon baking powder
- 1/2 teaspoon baking soda
- 1/2 teaspoon salt
- 1 teaspoon ground cinnamon
- 1/2 teaspoon ground ginger
- 1/4 teaspoon ground cloves
- 1/4 teaspoon ground nutmeg
- 1/2 cup unsalted butter (softened)
- 1 cup granulated sugar
- 2 large eggs
- 1/2 cup coconut milk (or regular milk)
- 1/4 cup crushed pineapple, drained
- 1/4 cup shredded coconut
- 1 teaspoon vanilla extract

For the Frosting:

- 1/2 cup unsalted butter (softened)
- 2 cups powdered sugar
- 1/4 cup coconut milk (or regular milk)
- 1/2 teaspoon vanilla extract
- 1/2 cup shredded coconut (for garnish)

Instructions:

1. **Preheat Oven and Prepare Pan:**
   - Preheat your oven to 350°F (175°C).
   - Line a 12-cup muffin tin with paper liners or lightly grease it.
2. **Prepare the Cupcake Batter:**
   - In a medium bowl, whisk together the flour, baking powder, baking soda, salt, cinnamon, ginger, cloves, and nutmeg.
   - In a large bowl, beat the softened butter and granulated sugar until light and fluffy.
   - Add the eggs one at a time, beating well after each addition.
   - Mix in the vanilla extract.
   - Gradually add the dry ingredients to the butter mixture, alternating with the coconut milk. Begin and end with the dry ingredients. Mix until just combined.

- Fold in the crushed pineapple and shredded coconut.
3. **Fill the Cupcake Liners:**
   - Divide the batter evenly among the 12 cupcake liners, filling each about 2/3 full.
4. **Bake:**
   - Bake in the preheated oven for 18-20 minutes, or until a toothpick inserted into the center of a cupcake comes out clean.
   - Allow the cupcakes to cool in the pan for 5 minutes before transferring them to a wire rack to cool completely.
5. **Prepare the Frosting:**
   - In a medium bowl, beat the softened butter until creamy.
   - Gradually add the powdered sugar, beating on low speed until combined.
   - Add the coconut milk and vanilla extract, and beat on high speed until the frosting is light and fluffy.
   - If the frosting is too thick, add a little more coconut milk; if it's too thin, add more powdered sugar.
6. **Frost the Cupcakes:**
   - Once the cupcakes are completely cooled, frost them with the coconut frosting using a spatula or piping bag.
   - Garnish with additional shredded coconut on top of each frosted cupcake.
7. **Serve:**
   - Enjoy the Island Spice Cupcakes as a delightful treat for any occasion.

Tips:

- **Spice Level:** Adjust the spices according to your taste preferences. You can add more or less of any spice to suit your liking.
- **Pineapple:** Ensure the pineapple is well-drained to avoid adding too much moisture to the batter.
- **Coconut Milk:** If you want a richer coconut flavor, you can use full-fat coconut milk in both the batter and the frosting.

Island Spice Cupcakes are a flavorful and exotic treat that combine the warmth of spices with tropical coconut and pineapple. They're perfect for adding a touch of the islands to your baking repertoire!

Tropical Fruit Salad with Lime Mint Dressing

Ingredients:

For the Fruit Salad:

- 2 cups pineapple chunks (fresh or canned, well-drained)
- 2 cups mango chunks (fresh or frozen, thawed)
- 1 cup kiwi, peeled and sliced
- 1 cup strawberries, hulled and sliced
- 1 banana, sliced
- 1 cup coconut chunks (fresh or dried coconut)
- Optional: 1/2 cup passion fruit pulp or diced papaya

For the Lime Mint Dressing:

- Juice of 2 limes
- 2 tablespoons honey or agave syrup (adjust to taste)
- 1 tablespoon finely chopped fresh mint leaves
- 1/2 teaspoon lime zest (optional, for extra lime flavor)

Instructions:

1. **Prepare the Fruit:**
   - In a large mixing bowl, combine the pineapple chunks, mango chunks, kiwi slices, strawberries, banana slices, and coconut chunks. If using passion fruit or papaya, add those as well.
2. **Prepare the Dressing:**
   - In a small bowl, whisk together the lime juice, honey or agave syrup, and lime zest (if using). Make sure the honey is well dissolved in the lime juice.
   - Stir in the finely chopped mint leaves.
3. **Combine and Serve:**
   - Drizzle the lime mint dressing over the fruit salad.
   - Gently toss the salad to coat the fruit evenly with the dressing. Be careful not to mash the fruit.
4. **Chill (Optional):**
   - For the best flavor, cover the fruit salad and refrigerate it for about 30 minutes before serving. This allows the flavors to meld together.
5. **Serve:**
   - Serve chilled as a refreshing side dish or dessert.

Tips:

- **Fruit Freshness:** Use ripe but firm fruit to ensure the best texture in the salad. Overripe fruit can become mushy.
- **Customization:** Feel free to customize the fruit selection based on what's in season or your personal preferences. Other tropical fruits like dragon fruit, guava, or starfruit can also be great additions.
- **Mint:** For a stronger mint flavor, you can muddle the mint leaves slightly before adding them to the dressing.

This Tropical Fruit Salad with Lime Mint Dressing is a light and flavorful dish that captures the essence of tropical paradise. The combination of sweet fruits and zesty lime mint dressing makes it a perfect addition to any summer meal or celebration.

Coconut Rice Krispies Treats

Ingredients:

- 6 cups Rice Krispies cereal
- 1/2 cup unsalted butter (1 stick)
- 1 package (10 oz) mini marshmallows (or 6 cups regular marshmallows)
- 1 cup sweetened shredded coconut (toasted or untoasted, based on preference)
- 1/2 teaspoon vanilla extract
- Optional: Additional shredded coconut for garnish

Instructions:

1. **Prepare the Pan:**
   - Grease a 9x13-inch baking dish or line it with parchment paper for easy removal of the treats.
2. **Toast the Coconut (Optional):**
   - If you prefer toasted coconut, spread the shredded coconut on a baking sheet and toast in a preheated oven at 350°F (175°C) for 5-7 minutes, or until golden brown. Stir occasionally to ensure even toasting. Let it cool before using.
3. **Melt Butter and Marshmallows:**
   - In a large saucepan, melt the butter over medium heat.
   - Once the butter is melted, add the mini marshmallows (or regular marshmallows) and stir continuously until completely melted and smooth.
   - Remove from heat and stir in the vanilla extract.
4. **Add Coconut and Cereal:**
   - Stir in the shredded coconut, mixing until evenly distributed.
   - Gently fold in the Rice Krispies cereal until well coated with the marshmallow mixture.
5. **Press into Pan:**
   - Transfer the mixture into the prepared baking dish.
   - Using a buttered spatula or wax paper, press the mixture firmly and evenly into the pan.
6. **Cool and Cut:**
   - Allow the treats to cool and set at room temperature for at least 30 minutes.
   - Once set, cut into squares or bars.
7. **Garnish (Optional):**
   - If desired, sprinkle additional shredded coconut on top of the treats before they fully set for extra texture and flavor.

Tips:

- **Sticky Hands:** To avoid sticky hands while pressing the mixture into the pan, lightly butter your hands or use a piece of wax paper.
- **Marshmallow Type:** Mini marshmallows melt more evenly, but you can use regular marshmallows if that's what you have on hand. Just cut them into smaller pieces to help them melt more quickly.
- **Storage:** Store the treats in an airtight container at room temperature. They are best enjoyed within a week.

Coconut Rice Krispies Treats offer a delightful combination of crisp cereal and chewy marshmallows with a hint of tropical coconut. They're easy to make and sure to be a hit with both kids and adults alike!

Mango and Sticky Rice Spring Rolls

Ingredients:

For the Sticky Rice:

- 1 cup glutinous (sticky) rice
- 1 1/4 cups coconut milk
- 1/4 cup granulated sugar
- 1/4 teaspoon salt

For the Spring Rolls:

- 6-8 rice paper wrappers
- 2 ripe mangos, peeled, pitted, and sliced into thin strips
- Fresh mint leaves (optional, for garnish)
- Toasted sesame seeds or shredded coconut (optional, for garnish)

For Serving:

- Sweetened coconut sauce (optional, for drizzling or dipping)
- Additional mango slices or fruit for garnish

Instructions:

1. **Prepare the Sticky Rice:**
    - Rinse the sticky rice under cold water until the water runs clear.
    - Soak the sticky rice in cold water for 30 minutes, then drain.
    - In a saucepan, combine the drained rice, coconut milk, sugar, and salt.
    - Bring to a boil, then reduce heat to low and simmer, covered, for about 15-20 minutes or until the rice is tender and the liquid is absorbed. Stir occasionally to prevent sticking.
    - Remove from heat and let it cool to room temperature.
2. **Prepare the Spring Rolls:**
    - Fill a shallow dish with warm water. Dip one rice paper wrapper into the water for about 10-15 seconds, or until it becomes pliable. Remove and lay it flat on a clean surface.
    - Place a small amount of sticky rice in the center of the rice paper, leaving some space on the sides for folding.
    - Arrange a few strips of mango on top of the sticky rice.
    - If using, place a few mint leaves on top for added flavor.
    - Fold the sides of the rice paper over the filling, then carefully roll it up from the bottom, tucking in the sides as you go. Repeat with the remaining wrappers and filling.

3. **Garnish and Serve:**
    - Arrange the spring rolls on a serving platter.
    - Garnish with toasted sesame seeds or shredded coconut if desired.
    - Serve with sweetened coconut sauce for drizzling or dipping, and additional mango slices or fruit on the side.

Tips:

- **Rice Paper Wrappers:** Make sure the rice paper is just soft enough to handle but not too mushy. Over-soaking can cause the wrappers to tear.
- **Sticky Rice:** Ensure the sticky rice is cool enough to handle but still pliable. If it becomes too firm, you can gently reheat it with a splash of coconut milk.
- **Garnishing:** Fresh mint leaves add a nice touch of flavor and color, but they are optional.

Mango and Sticky Rice Spring Rolls offer a refreshing and unique way to enjoy the classic Thai dessert. They are perfect for a light dessert, a summer treat, or a creative addition to a party spread.

Rum Punch Gelato

Ingredients:

For the Gelato Base:

- 1 cup coconut milk (full-fat for creaminess)
- 1 cup heavy cream
- 3/4 cup granulated sugar
- 1/2 cup light rum
- 1/4 cup freshly squeezed orange juice
- 1/4 cup freshly squeezed lime juice
- 1/4 cup pineapple juice
- 1 teaspoon vanilla extract
- Optional: 1 tablespoon grated orange zest
- Optional: 1 tablespoon grated lime zest

For Garnish (Optional):

- Fresh fruit (such as pineapple or orange slices)
- Mint leaves
- Additional grated citrus zest

Instructions:

1. **Prepare the Gelato Base:**
   - In a large mixing bowl, combine the coconut milk, heavy cream, and granulated sugar. Whisk until the sugar is fully dissolved.
   - Stir in the light rum, orange juice, lime juice, pineapple juice, and vanilla extract. Mix well.
   - If using, add the grated orange and lime zest to enhance the citrus flavor.
2. **Chill the Mixture:**
   - Cover the bowl and refrigerate the mixture for at least 1 hour, or until thoroughly chilled. This step helps the mixture churn more smoothly.
3. **Churn the Gelato:**
   - Pour the chilled mixture into an ice cream maker and churn according to the manufacturer's instructions. This usually takes about 20-25 minutes, or until the gelato reaches a creamy, soft-serve consistency.
4. **Freeze:**
   - Transfer the churned gelato to an airtight container and smooth the top. Freeze for at least 2 hours, or until firm.
5. **Serve:**
   - Scoop the Rum Punch Gelato into bowls or cones. Garnish with fresh fruit slices, mint leaves, or additional citrus zest if desired.

6. **Store:**
    - Store any leftover gelato in the freezer in an airtight container. Let it sit at room temperature for a few minutes before serving if it becomes too hard.

Tips:

- **Rum:** Adjust the amount of rum to your taste. If you prefer a stronger rum flavor, you can increase the quantity slightly. For a non-alcoholic version, you can omit the rum, though the texture might be slightly different.
- **Texture:** Gelato should be smooth and creamy. If you don't have an ice cream maker, you can freeze the mixture in a shallow dish, stirring every 30 minutes to break up ice crystals until fully frozen.
- **Flavor Variations:** Feel free to experiment with other fruit juices or add-ins, such as a splash of grenadine or a few fresh berries, to customize the flavor to your liking.

Rum Punch Gelato brings the vibrant flavors of a tropical cocktail into a creamy, frozen dessert, making it a perfect treat for warm weather or festive occasions. Enjoy the rich and refreshing taste!

Papaya Coconut Cheesecake Bars

Ingredients:

For the Crust:

- 1 1/2 cups graham cracker crumbs (about 12 graham crackers)
- 1/4 cup granulated sugar
- 1/2 cup unsalted butter (melted)

For the Cheesecake Filling:

- 16 oz (450 g) cream cheese (softened)
- 1 cup granulated sugar
- 3 large eggs
- 1 cup pureed fresh papaya (see tips below)
- 1/2 cup coconut milk (full-fat for creaminess)
- 1 teaspoon vanilla extract
- 1/2 cup shredded coconut (sweetened or unsweetened, as preferred)

For the Topping (Optional):

- 1/2 cup shredded coconut (toasted or untoasted)
- Fresh papaya slices or chunks
- Mint leaves (for garnish)

Instructions:

1. **Prepare the Crust:**
   - Preheat your oven to 325°F (160°C).
   - In a medium bowl, mix the graham cracker crumbs, granulated sugar, and melted butter until well combined.
   - Press the mixture evenly into the bottom of a 9x13-inch baking dish or a similarly sized pan lined with parchment paper. Use the back of a spoon or the bottom of a glass to press it down firmly.
   - Bake the crust in the preheated oven for 8-10 minutes, or until lightly golden. Remove from the oven and let cool while you prepare the filling.
2. **Prepare the Cheesecake Filling:**
   - In a large bowl, beat the softened cream cheese until smooth and creamy.
   - Gradually add the granulated sugar and continue to beat until well combined and smooth.
   - Add the eggs one at a time, beating well after each addition.
   - Mix in the pureed papaya, coconut milk, and vanilla extract until fully incorporated.

- Fold in the shredded coconut.
3. **Assemble and Bake:**
    - Pour the cheesecake filling over the cooled crust and smooth the top with a spatula.
    - Bake in the preheated oven for 30-35 minutes, or until the center is set and the edges are slightly puffed and golden.
    - Turn off the oven and let the cheesecake bars cool in the oven with the door slightly ajar for about 1 hour. This helps prevent cracking.
    - Once cooled, refrigerate for at least 4 hours, or overnight, to fully set and chill.
4. **Add Topping and Serve:**
    - If using, sprinkle the top of the bars with toasted shredded coconut and arrange fresh papaya slices or chunks for garnish.
    - Cut into bars and serve chilled. Garnish with mint leaves if desired.
5. **Store:**
    - Store any leftover cheesecake bars in an airtight container in the refrigerator for up to 5 days.

Tips:

- **Papaya Puree:** To make papaya puree, peel and seed a ripe papaya, cut it into chunks, and blend until smooth. You can also use canned papaya puree if fresh is not available.
- **Shredded Coconut:** You can use sweetened or unsweetened shredded coconut based on your preference. Toasted coconut adds an extra layer of flavor and texture.
- **Crust Alternatives:** If you prefer, you can use a different type of crust, such as a crushed cookie crust, for variation.

Papaya Coconut Cheesecake Bars offer a creamy and tropical twist on traditional cheesecake, making them a perfect dessert for summer gatherings or any time you want to enjoy a taste of the tropics.

Pineapple Gingerbread Cookies

Ingredients:

For the Cookies:

- 2 1/4 cups all-purpose flour
- 1/2 teaspoon baking soda
- 1/2 teaspoon baking powder
- 1 tablespoon ground ginger
- 1 tablespoon ground cinnamon
- 1/2 teaspoon ground cloves
- 1/4 teaspoon ground nutmeg
- 1/2 teaspoon salt
- 1/2 cup unsalted butter (softened)
- 1/2 cup brown sugar (packed)
- 1/4 cup granulated sugar
- 1/2 cup unsweetened pineapple puree (see tips below)
- 1 large egg
- 1/4 cup molasses
- 1 teaspoon vanilla extract

For the Icing (Optional):

- 1 cup powdered sugar
- 2 tablespoons milk
- 1/2 teaspoon vanilla extract

Instructions:

1. **Prepare the Dough:**
    - In a medium bowl, whisk together the flour, baking soda, baking powder, ginger, cinnamon, cloves, nutmeg, and salt.
    - In a large bowl, beat the softened butter with the brown sugar and granulated sugar until light and fluffy.
    - Add the pineapple puree, egg, molasses, and vanilla extract. Mix until well combined.
    - Gradually add the dry ingredients to the wet ingredients, mixing until just combined. The dough will be slightly soft but manageable.
2. **Chill the Dough:**
    - Divide the dough in half, wrap each portion in plastic wrap, and refrigerate for at least 1 hour. Chilling helps the dough firm up and makes it easier to roll out.
3. **Preheat Oven and Prepare Baking Sheets:**
    - Preheat your oven to 350°F (175°C).

- Line baking sheets with parchment paper or silicone baking mats.
4. **Roll Out and Cut Cookies:**
    - On a lightly floured surface, roll out one portion of the dough to about 1/4 inch thickness.
    - Use cookie cutters to cut out desired shapes and transfer them to the prepared baking sheets. Re-roll and cut the remaining dough as needed.
    - Repeat with the second portion of dough.
5. **Bake:**
    - Bake in the preheated oven for 8-10 minutes, or until the edges are firm and slightly golden.
    - Allow the cookies to cool on the baking sheets for 5 minutes before transferring them to wire racks to cool completely.
6. **Prepare the Icing (Optional):**
    - In a small bowl, mix together the powdered sugar, milk, and vanilla extract until smooth. Adjust the consistency with more milk or powdered sugar if needed.
    - Once the cookies are completely cooled, pipe or spread the icing onto the cookies as desired.
7. **Serve and Store:**
    - Serve the cookies once the icing has set.
    - Store in an airtight container at room temperature for up to 1 week.

Tips:

- **Pineapple Puree:** To make pineapple puree, blend fresh pineapple chunks or use canned pineapple (drained) until smooth. Ensure the puree is not too watery; if needed, drain excess liquid.
- **Rolling Dough:** If the dough becomes too soft while rolling, return it to the refrigerator for a few minutes to chill and firm up.
- **Icing Variations:** You can add food coloring to the icing for a festive touch or use different types of sprinkles or edible decorations.

Pineapple Gingerbread Cookies offer a unique and tropical twist on traditional gingerbread, combining warm spices with sweet pineapple flavor for a delicious and memorable treat.

Caribbean Chocolate Cake

Ingredients:

For the Cake:

- 1 3/4 cups all-purpose flour
- 1 1/2 teaspoons baking powder
- 1 1/2 teaspoons baking soda
- 1/2 teaspoon salt
- 1/2 cup unsweetened cocoa powder
- 1 cup granulated sugar
- 1 cup brown sugar (packed)
- 1/2 cup vegetable oil
- 1/2 cup buttermilk (or milk with 1 tablespoon lemon juice or vinegar)
- 1/2 cup coconut milk
- 2 large eggs
- 1 teaspoon vanilla extract
- 1/4 cup dark rum (optional, for a Caribbean twist)

For the Chocolate Ganache Frosting:

- 1 cup heavy cream
- 8 oz (225 g) semisweet or bittersweet chocolate, chopped
- 2 tablespoons unsalted butter
- 1 tablespoon dark rum (optional)

For Garnish (Optional):

- Toasted shredded coconut
- Chocolate shavings or curls
- Fresh fruit (such as pineapple or mango slices)

Instructions:

1. **Preheat Oven and Prepare Pans:**
    - Preheat your oven to 350°F (175°C).
    - Grease and flour two 9-inch round cake pans or line them with parchment paper.
2. **Make the Cake Batter:**
    - In a medium bowl, sift together the flour, baking powder, baking soda, salt, and cocoa powder.
    - In a large bowl, whisk together the granulated sugar, brown sugar, and oil until well combined.
    - Add the eggs one at a time, beating well after each addition.

- Stir in the vanilla extract, buttermilk, and coconut milk until smooth.
  - Gradually add the dry ingredients to the wet ingredients, mixing until just combined. If using, fold in the dark rum.
  - Divide the batter evenly between the prepared cake pans.
3. **Bake the Cake:**
   - Bake in the preheated oven for 25-30 minutes, or until a toothpick inserted into the center comes out clean.
   - Allow the cakes to cool in the pans for 10 minutes before transferring to a wire rack to cool completely.
4. **Prepare the Ganache Frosting:**
   - In a small saucepan, heat the heavy cream over medium heat until it just begins to simmer.
   - Remove from heat and add the chopped chocolate. Let it sit for 2-3 minutes, then stir until smooth.
   - Stir in the butter and dark rum (if using). Continue to stir until the ganache is glossy and smooth.
   - Let the ganache cool to room temperature before using. It will thicken as it cools.
5. **Assemble and Frost the Cake:**
   - If the cakes have domed tops, level them with a knife to create a flat surface.
   - Place one cake layer on a serving plate or cake stand. Spread a layer of ganache on top.
   - Place the second cake layer on top and spread the remaining ganache evenly over the top and sides of the cake.
6. **Garnish and Serve:**
   - Garnish with toasted shredded coconut, chocolate shavings or curls, and fresh fruit if desired.
   - Allow the cake to set for at least 30 minutes before slicing.
7. **Store:**
   - Store the cake in an airtight container at room temperature for up to 3 days or refrigerate for up to 1 week.

Tips:

- **Rum:** The dark rum adds a rich, Caribbean flavor to the cake. If you prefer a non-alcoholic version, you can omit it.
- **Ganache Consistency:** If the ganache is too thick after cooling, gently reheat it in the microwave or over a double boiler until it reaches the desired consistency.
- **Coconut:** For extra coconut flavor, you can also add shredded coconut to the cake batter or sprinkle it on top as a garnish.

Caribbean Chocolate Cake offers a delightful combination of rich chocolate and tropical flavors, making it a perfect dessert for any occasion. Enjoy the tropical twist on a classic chocolate cake!

Mango Lime Bars

Ingredients:

For the Crust:

- 1 1/2 cups all-purpose flour
- 1/2 cup granulated sugar
- 1/2 cup unsalted butter (cold and cubed)
- 1/4 teaspoon salt

For the Mango Lime Filling:

- 1 cup mango puree (see tips below)
- 1/2 cup freshly squeezed lime juice (about 4-5 limes)
- 1 tablespoon lime zest
- 4 large eggs
- 1 cup granulated sugar
- 1/4 cup all-purpose flour
- 1/4 teaspoon salt

For Garnish (Optional):

- Powdered sugar
- Lime zest
- Fresh mango slices or mint leaves

Instructions:

1. **Prepare the Crust:**
    - Preheat your oven to 350°F (175°C).
    - Grease and line an 8x8-inch or 9x9-inch baking dish with parchment paper, leaving some overhang for easy removal.
2. **Make the Crust:**
    - In a medium bowl, combine the flour, granulated sugar, and salt.
    - Cut in the cold, cubed butter using a pastry cutter, fork, or your fingers until the mixture resembles coarse crumbs.
    - Press the mixture evenly into the bottom of the prepared baking dish.
3. **Bake the Crust:**
    - Bake in the preheated oven for 15-20 minutes, or until the edges are lightly golden. Remove from the oven and let cool slightly while you prepare the filling.
4. **Prepare the Mango Lime Filling:**
    - In a large bowl, whisk together the mango puree, lime juice, lime zest, and eggs until smooth.

- Add the granulated sugar, flour, and salt, and whisk until fully combined and smooth.
5. **Assemble and Bake:**
    - Pour the mango lime filling over the partially cooled crust.
    - Bake in the preheated oven for 25-30 minutes, or until the filling is set and the edges are slightly golden. The center may still be slightly jiggly but will firm up as it cools.
6. **Cool and Serve:**
    - Allow the bars to cool completely in the pan on a wire rack.
    - Once cooled, refrigerate for at least 2 hours to fully set and chill.
    - Lift the bars out of the pan using the parchment paper overhang and cut into squares.
7. **Garnish and Serve:**
    - Before serving, dust the top with powdered sugar if desired.
    - Garnish with additional lime zest, fresh mango slices, or mint leaves for a decorative touch.
8. **Store:**
    - Store the bars in an airtight container in the refrigerator for up to 5 days. They can also be frozen for up to 2 months. Thaw in the refrigerator before serving.

Tips:

- **Mango Puree:** To make mango puree, blend fresh mango chunks until smooth. You can also use canned or frozen mango puree, but ensure it's thawed and well-drained if using frozen.
- **Lime Juice:** For the freshest flavor, use freshly squeezed lime juice rather than bottled.
- **Texture:** If the filling seems too runny before baking, add a bit more flour to thicken it, but it should set properly during baking.

Mango Lime Bars offer a bright, tropical twist on traditional lemon bars, with a delicious balance of sweet mango and tart lime. They're a perfect treat for warm weather or any time you want a refreshing, fruity dessert. Enjoy!

Coconut Lime Cheesecake

Ingredients:

For the Crust:

- 1 1/2 cups graham cracker crumbs (about 12 graham crackers)
- 1/2 cup shredded coconut (sweetened or unsweetened, depending on preference)
- 1/4 cup granulated sugar
- 1/2 cup unsalted butter (melted)

For the Cheesecake Filling:

- 16 oz (450 g) cream cheese (softened)
- 1 cup granulated sugar
- 1/2 cup coconut milk (full-fat)
- 1/4 cup sour cream
- 3 large eggs
- 1/4 cup freshly squeezed lime juice (about 2 limes)
- 2 tablespoons lime zest
- 1 teaspoon vanilla extract
- 1/2 cup shredded coconut (for mixing into the filling)

For the Coconut Lime Topping (Optional):

- 1/2 cup sour cream
- 2 tablespoons granulated sugar
- 1 tablespoon freshly squeezed lime juice
- 1/4 cup shredded coconut (toasted or untoasted)

Instructions:

1. **Preheat Oven and Prepare Pan:**
   - Preheat your oven to 325°F (160°C).
   - Grease and line a 9-inch springform pan with parchment paper or aluminum foil. If using parchment, make sure it extends up the sides of the pan for easy removal.
2. **Prepare the Crust:**
   - In a medium bowl, combine the graham cracker crumbs, shredded coconut, granulated sugar, and melted butter. Mix until well combined.
   - Press the mixture evenly into the bottom of the prepared springform pan. Use the back of a spoon or the bottom of a glass to pack it down firmly.
   - Bake in the preheated oven for 8-10 minutes, or until slightly golden. Remove from the oven and let cool while preparing the filling.

3. **Prepare the Cheesecake Filling:**
   - In a large mixing bowl, beat the softened cream cheese until smooth and creamy.
   - Gradually add the granulated sugar and continue to beat until well combined and smooth.
   - Mix in the coconut milk and sour cream until fully incorporated.
   - Add the eggs one at a time, beating well after each addition.
   - Stir in the lime juice, lime zest, and vanilla extract.
   - Fold in the shredded coconut.
4. **Assemble and Bake:**
   - Pour the cheesecake filling over the cooled crust in the springform pan. Smooth the top with a spatula.
   - Place the springform pan on a baking sheet to catch any drips.
   - Bake in the preheated oven for 50-60 minutes, or until the center is set and the edges are slightly puffed. The center may still be slightly jiggly but will firm up as it cools.
   - Turn off the oven and let the cheesecake cool in the oven with the door slightly ajar for about 1 hour. This helps prevent cracking.
5. **Prepare the Topping (Optional):**
   - In a small bowl, mix together the sour cream, granulated sugar, and lime juice until smooth.
   - Spread the topping over the cooled cheesecake.
   - Sprinkle with shredded coconut.
6. **Chill and Serve:**
   - Refrigerate the cheesecake for at least 4 hours, or overnight, to fully set and chill.
   - Remove from the springform pan and transfer to a serving platter.
   - Garnish with additional lime zest or fresh lime slices if desired.
7. **Store:**
   - Store any leftover cheesecake in an airtight container in the refrigerator for up to 1 week.

Tips:

- **Shredded Coconut:** Toasted shredded coconut can add a nice texture and flavor contrast. To toast, spread it on a baking sheet and bake at 350°F (175°C) for 5-7 minutes, or until golden brown, stirring occasionally.
- **Lime Juice:** Freshly squeezed lime juice provides the best flavor. If you prefer a more pronounced lime taste, you can adjust the amount of lime juice to your liking.
- **Crust Alternatives:** If you prefer, you can use a different type of crust, such as a crushed cookie crust or a graham cracker and nut crust.

Coconut Lime Cheesecake combines creamy cheesecake with vibrant lime and tropical coconut flavors, making it a delicious and refreshing dessert. Enjoy!

Tropical Sorbet Sundaes

Ingredients:

For the Sorbets:

- 2 cups mango sorbet
- 2 cups pineapple sorbet
- 2 cups coconut sorbet

For the Toppings:

- 1 cup fresh pineapple chunks
- 1 cup fresh mango chunks
- 1 banana, sliced
- 1/4 cup shredded coconut (toasted or untoasted)
- 1/4 cup chopped macadamia nuts or toasted almonds
- Fresh mint leaves (for garnish)
- Optional: A drizzle of honey or agave syrup

Instructions:

1. **Prepare the Sorbet:**
    - If you're making your own sorbet, follow the recipe or instructions for your sorbet maker. Alternatively, you can use store-bought sorbets for convenience.
2. **Assemble the Sundaes:**
    - In serving glasses or bowls, start by scooping a layer of mango sorbet at the bottom.
    - Add a layer of pineapple sorbet on top of the mango sorbet.
    - Follow with a layer of coconut sorbet.
    - Repeat the layers if you have taller glasses or bowls and prefer more layers.
3. **Add the Fresh Fruits:**
    - Top the sorbet layers with fresh pineapple chunks, mango chunks, and banana slices.
4. **Add Toppings:**
    - Sprinkle the sundaes with shredded coconut and chopped macadamia nuts or almonds.
    - Garnish with fresh mint leaves.
5. **Optional Drizzle:**
    - For added sweetness, you can drizzle a bit of honey or agave syrup over the top.
6. **Serve:**
    - Serve immediately for a refreshing and cold treat, or place in the freezer for a short time if the sorbet needs to firm up before serving.

Tips:

- **Sorbet Varieties:** Feel free to mix and match different tropical sorbets based on your preference or what's available.
- **Fruit Freshness:** Use ripe and fresh fruits for the best flavor and texture.
- **Make Ahead:** If preparing ahead of time, keep the assembled sundaes in the freezer but let them sit at room temperature for a few minutes before serving to soften slightly.

Tropical Sorbet Sundaes are a fun and customizable dessert that highlights the vibrant flavors of tropical fruits. Enjoy this refreshing treat any time you need a cool and fruity dessert!

Spiced Plantain Muffins

Ingredients:

For the Muffins:

- 2 ripe plantains (peeled and mashed)
- 1/2 cup granulated sugar
- 1/4 cup brown sugar (packed)
- 1/2 cup unsalted butter (melted)
- 1/4 cup plain yogurt or buttermilk
- 2 large eggs
- 1 teaspoon vanilla extract
- 1 1/2 cups all-purpose flour
- 1 teaspoon baking powder
- 1/2 teaspoon baking soda
- 1/2 teaspoon salt
- 1 teaspoon ground cinnamon
- 1/2 teaspoon ground nutmeg
- 1/4 teaspoon ground cloves
- Optional: 1/2 cup chopped nuts (such as walnuts or pecans) or chocolate chips

For the Topping (Optional):

- 2 tablespoons granulated sugar
- 1/2 teaspoon ground cinnamon

Instructions:

1. **Preheat Oven and Prepare Muffin Tin:**
    - Preheat your oven to 350°F (175°C).
    - Line a 12-cup muffin tin with paper liners or lightly grease the cups.
2. **Prepare the Muffin Batter:**
    - In a large bowl, whisk together the mashed plantains, granulated sugar, brown sugar, melted butter, yogurt (or buttermilk), eggs, and vanilla extract until smooth and well combined.
    - In another bowl, sift together the flour, baking powder, baking soda, salt, cinnamon, nutmeg, and cloves.
    - Gradually add the dry ingredients to the wet ingredients, mixing until just combined. Be careful not to overmix.
    - If using, fold in the chopped nuts or chocolate chips.
3. **Fill Muffin Cups:**
    - Divide the batter evenly among the 12 muffin cups, filling each about 2/3 full.
4. **Prepare the Topping (Optional):**

- In a small bowl, mix together the granulated sugar and ground cinnamon.
- Sprinkle the cinnamon-sugar mixture evenly over the tops of the muffin batter.
5. **Bake the Muffins:**
    - Bake in the preheated oven for 18-22 minutes, or until a toothpick inserted into the center of a muffin comes out clean.
    - Allow the muffins to cool in the pan for 5 minutes before transferring them to a wire rack to cool completely.
6. **Serve and Store:**
    - Enjoy the muffins warm or at room temperature.
    - Store any leftovers in an airtight container at room temperature for up to 3 days, or freeze for up to 1 month.

Tips:

- **Ripeness of Plantains:** Use very ripe plantains for the best flavor and natural sweetness. They should be mostly black and soft to the touch.
- **Mashed Plantains:** Ensure the plantains are mashed smoothly for a consistent texture in the muffins.
- **Mix-Ins:** Feel free to experiment with other mix-ins like dried fruit, coconut flakes, or different types of nuts.

Spiced Plantain Muffins offer a delightful combination of tropical plantain and warming spices, making them a unique and tasty treat for any time of the day. Enjoy!

Rum and Raisin Bread Pudding

Ingredients:

For the Bread Pudding:

- 6 cups stale bread (such as brioche, challah, or French bread), cut into 1-inch cubes
- 1 cup raisins
- 1/2 cup dark rum
- 4 large eggs
- 2 1/2 cups whole milk
- 1/2 cup heavy cream
- 3/4 cup granulated sugar
- 1/2 cup packed brown sugar
- 1 teaspoon vanilla extract
- 1 teaspoon ground cinnamon
- 1/2 teaspoon ground nutmeg
- 1/4 teaspoon salt

For the Sauce (Optional):

- 1/2 cup heavy cream
- 1/4 cup dark rum
- 1/4 cup granulated sugar
- 1 tablespoon butter

Instructions:

1. **Prepare the Bread and Raisins:**
    - Preheat your oven to 350°F (175°C).
    - Place the bread cubes in a large mixing bowl.
    - In a small bowl, combine the raisins and dark rum. Let them soak for about 15-20 minutes to plump up.
2. **Make the Custard:**
    - In a separate large bowl, whisk together the eggs, whole milk, heavy cream, granulated sugar, brown sugar, vanilla extract, ground cinnamon, ground nutmeg, and salt until well combined.
3. **Assemble the Bread Pudding:**
    - Add the soaked raisins and rum to the bread cubes, and toss to combine.
    - Pour the custard mixture over the bread cubes, gently stirring to ensure all the bread is evenly coated. Let it sit for 10-15 minutes, allowing the bread to absorb the custard mixture.
4. **Bake the Bread Pudding:**

- Transfer the bread mixture to a greased 9x13-inch baking dish or a similar-sized dish.
- Bake in the preheated oven for 45-55 minutes, or until the pudding is set and the top is golden brown. A knife inserted into the center should come out clean.

5. **Prepare the Sauce (Optional):**
    - While the bread pudding is baking, prepare the sauce if desired.
    - In a small saucepan, combine the heavy cream, dark rum, granulated sugar, and butter.
    - Heat over medium heat, stirring occasionally, until the sugar is dissolved and the mixture is slightly thickened (about 5 minutes).
6. **Serve:**
    - Allow the bread pudding to cool slightly before serving. It can be served warm or at room temperature.
    - Drizzle with the rum sauce if using, or serve with a scoop of vanilla ice cream or a dollop of whipped cream.
7. **Store:**
    - Store any leftovers in an airtight container in the refrigerator for up to 3 days. Reheat before serving.

Tips:

- **Bread Choice:** Stale bread works best as it absorbs the custard mixture more effectively. Fresh bread can be dried out in the oven for a few minutes before using.
- **Raisin Alternatives:** You can use other dried fruits, like currants or chopped dried apricots, if you prefer.
- **Custard Consistency:** If the custard seems too thick, add a little more milk or cream to reach your desired consistency before baking.

Rum and Raisin Bread Pudding combines comforting bread pudding with the rich flavors of rum and raisins, making it a deliciously indulgent dessert. Enjoy!

Pineapple Coconut Bars

Ingredients:

For the Crust:

- 1 1/2 cups all-purpose flour
- 1/2 cup granulated sugar
- 1/4 teaspoon salt
- 1/2 cup unsalted butter (cold and cubed)

For the Filling:

- 1 cup crushed pineapple (canned, drained)
- 1 cup sweetened shredded coconut
- 1/2 cup granulated sugar
- 2 large eggs
- 1/4 cup all-purpose flour
- 1 teaspoon vanilla extract
- 1/4 teaspoon salt

For the Glaze (Optional):

- 1/2 cup powdered sugar
- 2 tablespoons pineapple juice (or milk)

Instructions:

1. **Preheat Oven and Prepare Pan:**
    - Preheat your oven to 350°F (175°C).
    - Grease and line an 8x8-inch baking dish with parchment paper, leaving some overhang for easy removal.
2. **Prepare the Crust:**
    - In a medium bowl, combine the flour, granulated sugar, and salt.
    - Cut in the cold, cubed butter using a pastry cutter, fork, or your fingers until the mixture resembles coarse crumbs.
    - Press the mixture evenly into the bottom of the prepared baking dish.
3. **Bake the Crust:**
    - Bake in the preheated oven for 12-15 minutes, or until the edges are lightly golden. Remove from the oven and set aside while preparing the filling.
4. **Prepare the Filling:**
    - In a large bowl, whisk together the granulated sugar, flour, and salt.
    - Add the eggs, one at a time, beating well after each addition.

- Stir in the drained crushed pineapple, shredded coconut, and vanilla extract until well combined.
5. **Assemble and Bake:**
    - Pour the pineapple coconut filling over the partially baked crust.
    - Return to the oven and bake for an additional 25-30 minutes, or until the filling is set and the top is lightly golden.
6. **Cool and Glaze:**
    - Allow the bars to cool completely in the pan on a wire rack.
    - If using, prepare the glaze by whisking together the powdered sugar and pineapple juice until smooth. Drizzle over the cooled bars.
7. **Cut and Serve:**
    - Lift the bars out of the pan using the parchment paper overhang and cut into squares or bars.
    - Serve at room temperature.
8. **Store:**
    - Store any leftovers in an airtight container at room temperature for up to 5 days. They can also be refrigerated for up to 1 week or frozen for up to 2 months.

Tips:

- **Draining Pineapple:** Ensure that the crushed pineapple is well-drained to prevent the filling from being too watery.
- **Shredded Coconut:** You can use sweetened or unsweetened shredded coconut depending on your preference for sweetness.
- **Additions:** Feel free to add chopped nuts, like macadamia nuts or almonds, to the filling for extra texture.

Pineapple Coconut Bars offer a tropical flavor and chewy texture that's sure to be a hit. Enjoy these delightful bars as a sweet treat any time of year!

Mango Sorbet Float

Ingredients:

- 2 cups mango sorbet (store-bought or homemade)
- 2 cups sparkling water, lemon-lime soda, or ginger ale (chilled)
- Fresh mint leaves (for garnish)
- Mango slices or fresh berries (for garnish, optional)

Instructions:

1. **Prepare Glasses:**
   - Chill your serving glasses in the freezer for a few minutes if you prefer them extra cold.
2. **Scoop the Sorbet:**
   - Scoop the mango sorbet into the chilled glasses, dividing it evenly. You can use 1 or 2 scoops per glass depending on your preference.
3. **Add the Fizzy Drink:**
   - Slowly pour the sparkling water, lemon-lime soda, or ginger ale over the sorbet. Pour gently to avoid too much fizz and overflow.
4. **Garnish and Serve:**
   - Garnish with fresh mint leaves and, if desired, mango slices or fresh berries.
   - Serve immediately with a straw or spoon.

Tips:

- **Sorbet Consistency:** If your sorbet is very hard, let it sit out for a few minutes to soften slightly before scooping.
- **Flavor Variations:** Experiment with different flavors of sorbet or soda to find your favorite combination. For example, raspberry sorbet with lemon-lime soda is a delicious alternative.
- **Add-Ins:** For extra fun, you can add a splash of fruit juice or a small amount of fruit liqueur (if serving adults) to the float.

Mango Sorbet Float is a delightful, easy-to-make treat that's perfect for cooling down on a hot day or adding a touch of tropical flair to your dessert menu. Enjoy!

Coconut Almond Energy Balls

Ingredients:

- 1 cup almonds (raw or toasted)
- 1 cup shredded coconut (unsweetened or sweetened, depending on preference)
- 1/2 cup dates (pitted)
- 1/4 cup almond butter or coconut oil
- 2 tablespoons honey or maple syrup
- 1 teaspoon vanilla extract
- A pinch of salt

Optional Add-Ins:

- 1 tablespoon chia seeds or flaxseeds
- 1/4 cup dark chocolate chips or cacao nibs
- 1/4 cup dried fruit (e.g., cranberries, raisins)

Instructions:

1. **Prepare the Almonds:**
   - Place the almonds in a food processor and pulse until finely chopped but not turned into almond flour. You want some texture, so be careful not to over-process.
2. **Blend the Mixture:**
   - Add the shredded coconut, dates, almond butter (or coconut oil), honey (or maple syrup), vanilla extract, and a pinch of salt to the food processor.
   - Process the mixture until it starts to come together and is sticky. If the mixture is too dry, you can add a little more almond butter or honey to help it bind.
3. **Incorporate Optional Add-Ins:**
   - If using, fold in chia seeds, flaxseeds, dark chocolate chips, or dried fruit.
4. **Form the Energy Balls:**
   - With your hands or a small cookie scoop, form the mixture into 1-inch balls and place them on a baking sheet or plate lined with parchment paper.
5. **Chill:**
   - Refrigerate the energy balls for at least 30 minutes to firm up.
6. **Serve and Store:**
   - Once chilled, the energy balls are ready to eat. Store them in an airtight container in the refrigerator for up to 1 week or freeze for up to 3 months.

Tips:

- **Date Substitution:** If you don't have dates, you can use other dried fruits like apricots or figs. Just make sure they are soft enough to blend easily.
- **Sweetness:** Adjust the sweetness to your preference by adding more or less honey or maple syrup.
- **Texture:** For a crunchier texture, consider adding a small amount of chopped nuts or seeds.

These Coconut Almond Energy Balls are a great way to enjoy a satisfying and healthful snack with minimal effort. They're perfect for grabbing on the go or packing in a lunchbox. Enjoy!

Passion Fruit Meringue Pie

Ingredients:

For the Pie Crust:

- 1 1/2 cups graham cracker crumbs
- 1/4 cup granulated sugar
- 1/2 cup unsalted butter (melted)

For the Passion Fruit Filling:

- 1 cup passion fruit juice (fresh or store-bought, preferably strained)
- 1 cup granulated sugar
- 1/4 cup cornstarch
- 1/4 teaspoon salt
- 1 1/2 cups water
- 4 large egg yolks
- 2 tablespoons unsalted butter
- 1 teaspoon vanilla extract

For the Meringue:

- 4 large egg whites
- 1/4 teaspoon cream of tartar
- 1/2 cup granulated sugar

Instructions:

1. **Prepare the Crust:**
   - Preheat your oven to 350°F (175°C).
   - In a medium bowl, combine the graham cracker crumbs, granulated sugar, and melted butter. Mix until the crumbs are evenly coated.
   - Press the mixture into the bottom and up the sides of a 9-inch pie dish.
   - Bake for 8-10 minutes or until lightly golden. Allow to cool while preparing the filling.
2. **Prepare the Passion Fruit Filling:**
   - In a medium saucepan, whisk together the granulated sugar, cornstarch, and salt.
   - Gradually whisk in the water and passion fruit juice.
   - Cook over medium heat, stirring constantly, until the mixture starts to thicken and comes to a boil.
   - Reduce the heat to low and cook for an additional 1-2 minutes, continuing to stir, until the mixture is thickened.

- In a small bowl, whisk the egg yolks. Gradually add a small amount of the hot passion fruit mixture to the egg yolks to temper them, then whisk the tempered yolks back into the saucepan.
- Continue to cook for 2-3 more minutes, stirring constantly.
- Remove from heat and stir in the butter and vanilla extract.
- Pour the filling into the prepared graham cracker crust and smooth the top.

3. **Prepare the Meringue:**
   - In a clean, dry bowl, beat the egg whites and cream of tartar with an electric mixer on medium speed until soft peaks form.
   - Gradually add the granulated sugar, beating on high speed until stiff, glossy peaks form.

4. **Assemble and Bake:**
   - Spoon the meringue over the passion fruit filling, spreading it to the edges of the crust and creating peaks and swirls.
   - Bake in the preheated oven for 10-12 minutes, or until the meringue is golden brown.

5. **Cool and Serve:**
   - Allow the pie to cool completely at room temperature before serving. This helps the filling to set properly.

6. **Store:**
   - Store any leftovers in the refrigerator for up to 3 days. The pie is best enjoyed within a day or two for optimal freshness.

Tips:

- **Passion Fruit Juice:** If using fresh passion fruit, strain the juice to remove seeds and pulp. You can also use store-bought passion fruit juice, but make sure it's 100% juice for the best flavor.
- **Meringue:** Make sure the bowl and beaters are completely clean and dry to ensure the meringue whips properly.
- **Pie Crust:** You can substitute graham cracker crumbs with crushed vanilla wafers or even a shortbread cookie crust if preferred.

Passion Fruit Meringue Pie offers a vibrant, tropical twist on a classic dessert, making it a perfect choice for special occasions or a refreshing treat. Enjoy!

Tropical Fruit Crumble

Ingredients:

For the Filling:

- 3 cups mixed tropical fruits (such as mango, pineapple, papaya, and banana), peeled, chopped, and lightly tossed with a tablespoon of lemon or lime juice
- 1/4 cup granulated sugar (adjust based on the sweetness of the fruit)
- 1 tablespoon cornstarch
- 1 teaspoon vanilla extract
- 1/2 teaspoon ground cinnamon

For the Crumble Topping:

- 1 cup old-fashioned rolled oats
- 1/2 cup all-purpose flour
- 1/2 cup packed brown sugar
- 1/4 cup granulated sugar
- 1/2 teaspoon ground cinnamon
- 1/4 teaspoon salt
- 1/2 cup unsalted butter (cold and cubed)

Instructions:

1. **Preheat Oven:**
   - Preheat your oven to 350°F (175°C).
2. **Prepare the Fruit Filling:**
   - In a large bowl, combine the chopped tropical fruits, granulated sugar, cornstarch, vanilla extract, and ground cinnamon. Toss to combine and coat the fruit evenly.
   - Transfer the fruit mixture to a greased 8x8-inch baking dish or a similar-sized ovenproof dish.
3. **Prepare the Crumble Topping:**
   - In a medium bowl, mix together the rolled oats, all-purpose flour, brown sugar, granulated sugar, ground cinnamon, and salt.
   - Cut in the cold, cubed butter using a pastry cutter, fork, or your fingers until the mixture resembles coarse crumbs.
4. **Assemble the Crumble:**
   - Sprinkle the crumble topping evenly over the fruit filling in the baking dish.
5. **Bake the Crumble:**
   - Bake in the preheated oven for 35-45 minutes, or until the topping is golden brown and the fruit filling is bubbly and thickened.
6. **Cool and Serve:**
   - Allow the crumble to cool slightly before serving. It can be enjoyed warm or at room temperature.

- Serve on its own or with a scoop of vanilla ice cream or a dollop of whipped cream for extra indulgence.
7. **Store:**
   - Store any leftovers in an airtight container in the refrigerator for up to 3 days. Reheat before serving if desired.

Tips:

- **Fruit Selection:** You can use a mix of fresh or frozen tropical fruits. If using frozen fruit, thaw and drain excess moisture before using.
- **Sweetness Adjustment:** Adjust the amount of sugar based on the ripeness and sweetness of your fruit. Taste the fruit mixture before adding to the baking dish.
- **Topping Texture:** For a crunchier topping, consider adding a handful of chopped nuts, like almonds or cashews, to the crumble mixture.

Tropical Fruit Crumble brings the flavors of the tropics into a comforting dessert that's perfect for any occasion. Enjoy the sweet and tangy fruit with a buttery, crumbly topping!

Pina Colada Cupcakes

Ingredients:

For the Cupcakes:

- 1 1/2 cups all-purpose flour
- 1 cup granulated sugar
- 1 1/2 teaspoons baking powder
- 1/2 teaspoon baking soda
- 1/4 teaspoon salt
- 1/2 cup unsalted butter (room temperature)
- 1/2 cup crushed pineapple (drained)
- 1/4 cup coconut milk (or full-fat coconut cream)
- 2 large eggs
- 1 teaspoon vanilla extract
- 1/2 teaspoon coconut extract

For the Frosting:

- 1/2 cup unsalted butter (room temperature)
- 1/4 cup coconut milk (or full-fat coconut cream)
- 2 cups powdered sugar
- 1/2 teaspoon vanilla extract
- 1/2 teaspoon coconut extract

For Garnish (Optional):

- Sweetened shredded coconut
- Pineapple slices or maraschino cherries

Instructions:

1. **Preheat Oven:**
   - Preheat your oven to 350°F (175°C) and line a muffin tin with cupcake liners.
2. **Prepare the Cupcake Batter:**
   - In a medium bowl, whisk together the flour, sugar, baking powder, baking soda, and salt.
   - In a separate large bowl, beat the butter until creamy.
   - Add the eggs one at a time, beating well after each addition.
   - Mix in the vanilla extract, coconut extract, and crushed pineapple.
   - Gradually add the dry ingredients to the wet ingredients, alternating with the coconut milk, beginning and ending with the dry ingredients. Mix until just combined.

3. **Bake the Cupcakes:**
    - Divide the batter evenly among the cupcake liners, filling each about 2/3 full.
    - Bake for 18-22 minutes, or until a toothpick inserted into the center comes out clean.
    - Allow the cupcakes to cool in the tin for 5 minutes, then transfer them to a wire rack to cool completely.
4. **Prepare the Frosting:**
    - In a large bowl, beat the butter until creamy.
    - Gradually add the powdered sugar, beating on low speed until combined.
    - Mix in the coconut milk, vanilla extract, and coconut extract until the frosting is smooth and fluffy.
5. **Frost the Cupcakes:**
    - Once the cupcakes are completely cool, frost them with the coconut frosting using a piping bag or a spatula.
6. **Garnish:**
    - If desired, sprinkle the frosted cupcakes with sweetened shredded coconut.
    - Garnish with a small slice of pineapple or a maraschino cherry.
7. **Serve and Store:**
    - Serve the cupcakes immediately or store them in an airtight container at room temperature for up to 3 days or in the refrigerator for up to 5 days.

Tips:

- **Pineapple:** Make sure to drain the crushed pineapple well to avoid adding excess moisture to the batter.
- **Coconut Milk:** For a richer flavor, use full-fat coconut milk or coconut cream.
- **Decorations:** For an extra tropical touch, you can also add a small paper umbrella or a tiny cocktail stirrer to the cupcakes.

Pina Colada Cupcakes are a fun and flavorful way to enjoy the tropical taste of pina coladas in a bite-sized dessert. Enjoy!

Papaya Sorbet

Ingredients:

- 3 cups ripe papaya, peeled, seeded, and cut into chunks
- 1/2 cup granulated sugar (adjust to taste, depending on the sweetness of your papaya)
- 1/2 cup water
- 2 tablespoons lime juice (freshly squeezed)
- 1 teaspoon vanilla extract (optional)
- A pinch of salt

Instructions:

1. **Prepare the Papaya:**
   - Place the papaya chunks in a blender or food processor.
2. **Blend the Mixture:**
   - Add the granulated sugar, water, lime juice, and a pinch of salt to the blender.
   - Blend until smooth. Taste the mixture and adjust the sweetness if needed by adding more sugar. You can also add more lime juice if you prefer a tangier flavor.
3. **Chill the Mixture:**
   - Pour the papaya mixture into a bowl and chill in the refrigerator for at least 1 hour. This helps the sorbet freeze more evenly.
4. **Freeze the Sorbet:**
   - If using an ice cream maker:
     - Pour the chilled mixture into the ice cream maker and churn according to the manufacturer's instructions, usually for about 20-25 minutes, until it reaches a soft-serve consistency.
   - If not using an ice cream maker:
     - Pour the mixture into a shallow dish or freezer-safe container.
     - Place it in the freezer and stir every 30 minutes with a fork to break up ice crystals until the sorbet is fully frozen and has a light, fluffy texture. This process may take 2-3 hours.
5. **Serve:**
   - Scoop the sorbet into bowls or glasses.
   - Garnish with fresh mint leaves or a slice of papaya if desired.
6. **Store:**
   - Store any leftover sorbet in an airtight container in the freezer for up to 1 month. Let it sit at room temperature for a few minutes before serving to soften slightly.

Tips:

- **Ripeness of Papaya:** Use ripe papaya for the best flavor. It should be slightly soft to the touch and have a sweet aroma.
- **Adjusting Sweetness:** Adjust the amount of sugar based on the sweetness of your papaya. If the papaya is very sweet, you may need less sugar.

- **Lime Juice:** Lime juice adds a nice tang and helps balance the sweetness. You can also use lemon juice if preferred.

Papaya Sorbet is a light, fruity, and refreshing treat that showcases the tropical flavor of papaya in a simple and elegant way. Enjoy!

Tropical Coconut Flan

Ingredients:

For the Caramel Sauce:

- 3/4 cup granulated sugar
- 1/4 cup water

For the Flan:

- 1 can (14 oz) sweetened condensed milk
- 1 can (13.5 oz) coconut milk (full-fat for creaminess)
- 1 cup whole milk
- 4 large eggs
- 1/2 cup granulated sugar
- 1 teaspoon vanilla extract
- 1/2 cup shredded coconut (unsweetened or sweetened, based on preference)
- Pinch of salt

Instructions:

1. **Prepare the Caramel Sauce:**
   - In a medium saucepan, combine the granulated sugar and water.
   - Cook over medium heat, without stirring, until the sugar dissolves and turns a golden brown color, about 10 minutes.
   - Carefully pour the hot caramel into the bottom of a 9-inch round cake pan or flan dish, tilting the pan to spread it evenly. Set aside to cool and harden.
2. **Prepare the Flan Mixture:**
   - Preheat your oven to 350°F (175°C).
   - In a large bowl, whisk together the sweetened condensed milk, coconut milk, whole milk, eggs, granulated sugar, vanilla extract, and a pinch of salt until well combined.
   - Stir in the shredded coconut.
3. **Bake the Flan:**
   - Pour the flan mixture over the set caramel in the cake pan.
   - Place the cake pan in a larger baking dish. Fill the larger baking dish with hot water until it reaches halfway up the sides of the cake pan (this creates a water bath to ensure even cooking).
   - Bake in the preheated oven for 50-60 minutes, or until the flan is set and a knife inserted into the center comes out clean.
4. **Cool and Chill:**
   - Remove the cake pan from the water bath and let it cool to room temperature.

- Once cooled, cover and refrigerate for at least 4 hours, or overnight, to fully set and chill.
5. **Serve:**
    - To unmold the flan, run a knife around the edges of the pan to loosen it. Place a large plate over the pan and invert it to release the flan onto the plate, allowing the caramel to drizzle over the top.
    - Garnish with additional shredded coconut if desired.
6. **Store:**
    - Store any leftovers in the refrigerator for up to 3 days.

Tips:

- **Caramel:** Be careful when making caramel as it gets very hot. Use a heavy-bottomed saucepan to ensure even cooking.
- **Coconut Milk:** For a richer flavor, use full-fat coconut milk. If you prefer a lighter version, you can use light coconut milk.
- **Flan Texture:** The flan should be smooth and creamy. Avoid overbaking, as this can cause the flan to become tough or cracked.

Tropical Coconut Flan offers a delicious blend of creamy coconut and rich caramel, making it a memorable and satisfying dessert. Enjoy!

Mango and Coconut Panna Cotta

Ingredients:

For the Panna Cotta:

- 1 can (13.5 oz) coconut milk (full-fat for creaminess)
- 1 cup heavy cream
- 1/2 cup granulated sugar
- 1 teaspoon vanilla extract
- 1 packet (about 2 1/4 teaspoons) unflavored gelatin
- 1/4 cup cold water

For the Mango Sauce:

- 2 ripe mangoes, peeled and diced
- 1/4 cup granulated sugar
- 1 tablespoon lime juice
- 1 tablespoon water

Instructions:

1. **Prepare the Gelatin:**
    - In a small bowl, sprinkle the unflavored gelatin over the cold water and let it sit for about 5 minutes to bloom.
2. **Make the Panna Cotta Base:**
    - In a medium saucepan, combine the coconut milk, heavy cream, and granulated sugar. Heat over medium heat, stirring occasionally, until the mixture is hot and the sugar is dissolved (do not let it boil).
    - Remove from heat and stir in the vanilla extract.
    - Add the bloomed gelatin to the hot cream mixture and stir until the gelatin is completely dissolved.
3. **Chill the Panna Cotta:**
    - Pour the mixture into individual serving glasses or ramekins.
    - Refrigerate for at least 4 hours or until the panna cotta is set and firm.
4. **Prepare the Mango Sauce:**
    - In a blender or food processor, combine the diced mangoes, granulated sugar, lime juice, and water.
    - Blend until smooth. If the sauce is too thick, you can add a bit more water to reach the desired consistency.
5. **Serve:**
    - Once the panna cotta is set, spoon or drizzle the mango sauce over the top.
    - Garnish with fresh mint leaves or additional diced mango if desired.
6. **Store:**
    - Store any leftover panna cotta and mango sauce separately in the refrigerator for up to 2 days.

Tips:

- **Mango Ripeness:** Choose ripe mangoes for the best flavor. They should be soft to the touch and fragrant.
- **Gelatin:** Ensure the gelatin is fully dissolved in the hot cream mixture to avoid lumps. If the mixture cools before the gelatin is fully dissolved, gently reheat it.
- **Serving:** For an elegant touch, serve the panna cotta in clear glasses or ramekins to showcase the layers and colors.

Mango and Coconut Panna Cotta combines tropical flavors with a creamy texture, making it a refreshing and delightful dessert. Enjoy!

Caribbean Sweet Potato Pie

Ingredients:

For the Pie Crust:

- 1 1/2 cups all-purpose flour
- 1/4 cup granulated sugar
- 1/2 teaspoon salt
- 1/2 cup unsalted butter (cold and cubed)
- 1/4 cup cold water (more if needed)

For the Sweet Potato Filling:

- 2 cups cooked and mashed sweet potatoes (about 2 medium sweet potatoes)
- 3/4 cup granulated sugar
- 1/2 cup coconut milk (full-fat for richness)
- 1/4 cup heavy cream
- 2 large eggs
- 1 teaspoon vanilla extract
- 1 teaspoon ground cinnamon
- 1/2 teaspoon ground nutmeg
- 1/4 teaspoon ground allspice
- 1/4 teaspoon ground ginger
- 1/4 teaspoon salt

For Garnish (Optional):

- Whipped cream
- Toasted coconut flakes

Instructions:

1. **Prepare the Pie Crust:**
    - In a large bowl, whisk together the flour, sugar, and salt.
    - Cut in the cold, cubed butter using a pastry cutter, fork, or your fingers until the mixture resembles coarse crumbs.
    - Gradually add cold water, one tablespoon at a time, mixing until the dough comes together.
    - Form the dough into a disk, wrap in plastic wrap, and refrigerate for at least 30 minutes.
2. **Preheat Oven:**
    - Preheat your oven to 375°F (190°C).
3. **Roll Out and Fit the Pie Crust:**

- On a lightly floured surface, roll out the dough to fit a 9-inch pie dish.
- Transfer the rolled dough to the pie dish and gently press it into the bottom and sides. Trim any excess dough and crimp the edges.

4. **Prepare the Sweet Potato Filling:**
   - In a large bowl, combine the mashed sweet potatoes, granulated sugar, coconut milk, heavy cream, eggs, vanilla extract, ground cinnamon, ground nutmeg, ground allspice, ground ginger, and salt. Mix until smooth and well combined.
5. **Assemble the Pie:**
   - Pour the sweet potato filling into the prepared pie crust, smoothing the top with a spatula.
6. **Bake the Pie:**
   - Bake in the preheated oven for 45-50 minutes, or until the filling is set and a knife inserted into the center comes out clean.
   - If the crust starts to brown too quickly, cover the edges with foil to prevent burning.
7. **Cool and Serve:**
   - Allow the pie to cool to room temperature before serving.
   - Garnish with whipped cream and toasted coconut flakes if desired.
8. **Store:**
   - Store any leftovers in the refrigerator for up to 4 days.

Tips:

- **Sweet Potatoes:** Make sure the sweet potatoes are well-cooked and thoroughly mashed to ensure a smooth filling.
- **Spices:** Adjust the spices to your taste if you prefer a stronger or milder flavor.
- **Crust:** For a more flavorful crust, you can add a pinch of cinnamon or nutmeg to the flour mixture.

Caribbean Sweet Potato Pie offers a unique and delicious twist on a classic dessert, combining the creamy texture of sweet potatoes with aromatic spices and tropical flavors. Enjoy!

Pineapple Coconut Ice Cream Sandwiches

Ingredients:

For the Pineapple Coconut Cookies:

- 1 1/2 cups all-purpose flour
- 1/2 teaspoon baking powder
- 1/4 teaspoon baking soda
- 1/4 teaspoon salt
- 1/2 cup unsalted butter (room temperature)
- 1/2 cup granulated sugar
- 1/2 cup packed brown sugar
- 1 large egg
- 1 teaspoon vanilla extract
- 1/2 cup crushed pineapple (drained well)
- 1/2 cup sweetened shredded coconut

For the Coconut Ice Cream:

- 1 can (13.5 oz) coconut milk (full-fat)
- 1 cup heavy cream
- 3/4 cup granulated sugar
- 1 teaspoon vanilla extract
- 1/2 teaspoon coconut extract (optional)

Instructions:

1. **Prepare the Cookies:**
    - Preheat your oven to 350°F (175°C) and line two baking sheets with parchment paper.
    - In a medium bowl, whisk together the flour, baking powder, baking soda, and salt.
    - In a large bowl, cream together the butter, granulated sugar, and brown sugar until light and fluffy.
    - Beat in the egg and vanilla extract until well combined.
    - Gradually add the dry ingredients to the wet ingredients, mixing until just combined.
    - Fold in the crushed pineapple and shredded coconut.
    - Drop rounded tablespoons of dough onto the prepared baking sheets, spacing them about 2 inches apart.
    - Flatten each dough ball slightly with the back of a spoon or your fingers.
    - Bake for 10-12 minutes, or until the edges are golden brown.
    - Allow the cookies to cool on the baking sheets for 5 minutes before transferring them to a wire rack to cool completely.

2. **Make the Coconut Ice Cream:**
    - In a medium bowl, whisk together the coconut milk, heavy cream, granulated sugar, vanilla extract, and coconut extract until the sugar is dissolved.
    - Pour the mixture into an ice cream maker and churn according to the manufacturer's instructions, usually for about 20-25 minutes, until it reaches a soft-serve consistency.
    - Transfer the churned ice cream to a lidded container and freeze for at least 2 hours to firm up.
3. **Assemble the Ice Cream Sandwiches:**
    - Once the cookies are completely cooled and the ice cream is firm, scoop a generous amount of coconut ice cream onto the bottom of one cookie.
    - Top with a second cookie, gently pressing to sandwich the ice cream between the cookies.
    - Repeat with the remaining cookies and ice cream.
    - If desired, roll the edges of the ice cream sandwiches in additional shredded coconut for extra texture and flavor.
4. **Serve and Store:**
    - Serve the ice cream sandwiches immediately or place them in the freezer for up to 1 hour to firm up further.
    - Store any leftover sandwiches in an airtight container in the freezer for up to 1 week.

Tips:

- **Cookie Texture:** Ensure the cookies are completely cooled before assembling the sandwiches to prevent the ice cream from melting too quickly.
- **Ice Cream Consistency:** If you don't have an ice cream maker, you can freeze the coconut mixture in a container, stirring every 30 minutes for the first 2-3 hours to break up ice crystals until firm.

Pineapple Coconut Ice Cream Sandwiches are a fun and tropical twist on a classic dessert, combining the sweet flavors of pineapple and coconut with creamy, cool ice cream. Enjoy!